# MUSEUM QUALITY

**Edward A. Mero**
*Author*

For more information on
**Gallery of the Great Museums of the World**
**www.MuseumQualityFineArt.com**
**800.838.9885   954.227.8186**

I dedicate this book to all of the art enthusiasts who have come before me and will come after me. To Mike Lyons, who planted the seed for my "Museum Vision" 20 years ago—and to the many artists of the world who have their own visions and so much to share.

I would also like to acknowledge several individuals who were instrumental in bringing this book to fruition: Diane Secor, who helped with the early drafts and chose the title, Museum Quality; Jaime Prieto for layout and design; Claudia Zaik for excellent editing of the first draft; Lorelee Martin for final edit; and Dr. Aurora Hill (Heartstonepub.com) for ideas and moral support. Pamela Bouroncle (Pi'iLani) for motivation. I would also like to express my appreciation for the contributions made by all of the artists included in this book.

Finally, this book takes me one step closer to leaving a legacy for Diane, and my lovely daughters, Nicole and Jacqueline. Long Live the Arts…

# Museum Quality

Is the term, museum quality, overused? Not when it applies to works of art that truly meet the definition. Museum quality is used to describe works of such high caliber and importance; they are included in the collections of prestigious world-class museums. These works of art have been deemed to warrant a place in the pantheon of art history, so they can be shared with present and future generations. This book explores many different works of art, both original masterpieces and expert copies, and the artists who create them--all within the context of the museum quality designation.

# Renowned Art Copyists of the World's – Greatest Paintings

*Art Washes Away From "The Soul the Dust of Everyday Life"*

*Picasso*

Artists for centuries have practiced the art of copying masterpiece paintings of artists who created works of art before them. This is a way of paying homage to the masters of art. The talent and craftsmanship that goes into copying a work of art can be more daunting in some cases then creating the original artwork. This is because the copyist must use all of his or her skills to capture the essence of the original and the style and techniques utilized by the original creator. To many an artist that have explored this path, it becomes a rite of passage to bigger and better creative exploitations. The artist of centuries past created the masterpieces of yesterday for the enjoyment of today.

photographer, Bruno Morandi, (The Image Bank) Getty Images

**COPYIST ARTIST RE-CREATING A MASTERPIECE AT THE LOUVRE**

*Paris, France*

# Table of Contents

Renowned Art Copyists of the World's – Greatest Paintings.................................................7

CHAPTER ONE | **Why Own A Copy Of A Museum Painting?**...............................11

CHAPTER TWO | **Collecting And Enjoying Great Art Reproductions**.................15

CHAPTER THREE | **Forgers, Artists, Copyists:  What's The Difference?**............21

"There is no such thing as a fake...only fake experts and their fake labels.".............24

"The Fakes Progress" written by Tom Keating (1978)..........................................25

Dr. Martin Luther King Jr. Painting................................................................27

CHAPTER FOUR | **The Extraordinary Artists Of Prestige Fine Art**...................33

Artist from Italy..........................................................................................36

Artist from Hungry......................................................................................37

Artist from Belgium.....................................................................................38

Artist from USA..........................................................................................39

Artist from Brazil.........................................................................................40

CHAPTER FIVE | **Lesser-Known Versus Famous Masterpieces**.......................43

CHAPTER SIX | **Museum Quality Framing**....................................................49

CHAPTER SEVEN | **World Class Museums**....................................................53

The Metropolitan Museum Of Art, New York City...........................................59

The Louvre, Paris, France............................................................................65

The National Gallery of Art, Washington, D.C.................................................71

The Philadelphia Museum Of Art..................................................................77

The Art Institute of Chicago........................................................................83

The Frick Collection....................................................................................89

The Tate Gallery.........................................................................................97

The Barnes Collection...............................................................................103

The J. Paul Getty Museum.........................................................................109

Uffizi & Pitti Gallery..................................................................................115

CHAPTER EIGHT | **Prestige Fine Art Categories** .................................................. 121

    Impressionism .................................................................................. 123

    Old Master Old World ...................................................................... 131

    Romantic Classical Victorian ............................................................ 137

    Historical and Western ..................................................................... 145

    Americana ....................................................................................... 153

    Pastels ............................................................................................ 161

    Portraits .......................................................................................... 163

CHAPTER NINE | **Sculpture** ...................................................................... 173

    The Eleganza Collection .................................................................. 174

    Eric Stepeniewski ............................................................................ 175

    Masterpiece Investments – Lorenzo Ghiglieri ................................. 177

    Nilda Maria Comas ......................................................................... 178

    The Kiss Collection .......................................................................... 179

CHAPTER TEN | **Photography And Photorealism** ...................................... 181

    Michael Poirier ................................................................................ 183

CHAPTER ELEVEN | **Collecting Original Art** .............................................. 185

    Auction Houses: Sotheby's and Christie's ....................................... 188

    Galleries .......................................................................................... 188

CHAPTER TWELVE | **Our Art Collectors' Homes** ...................................... 189

    Highland Beach Home ..................................................................... 190

    Atlanta Home .................................................................................. 192

    London Home .................................................................................. 194

    Royal Palm Home ............................................................................ 196

    Sanctuary Home .............................................................................. 198

    Boca Raton Home ........................................................................... 200

    Victoria Park Home .......................................................................... 202

CHAPTER THIRTEEN | **Testimonial** ........................................................... 205

CHAPTER FOURTEEN | **Suggested Art Books and Movies** ........................ 209

    Suggested Movies ........................................................................... 212

CHAPTER FIFTEEN | **Prestige Fine Art's Museum-Inspired Vision** ............ 213

CHAPTER SIXTEEN | **Edward Mero** – *Prestige Fine Art* ............................ 227

# Why Own A Copy Of A Museum Painting?

THERE ARE MANY REASONS YOU MIGHT WANT TO OWN A COPY OF A FAMOUS MUSEUM PAINTING. MUSEUMS AROUND THE WORLD ARE VISITED BY THOUSANDS OF PEOPLE WHO ADMIRE GREAT WORKS OF ART, BUT MOST OF THESE DEVOTEES CANNOT AFFORD TO OWN AN ORIGINAL. AS A RESULT, THERE IS A LARGE MARKET FOR TOP-QUALITY COPIES OF WORLD-CLASS PAINTINGS, CREATED FOR THE EVERYDAY ENJOYMENT OF THE VIEWER. THESE ARE OFTEN BELOVED MASTERPIECES THAT PROVIDE A PERSONAL CONNECTION, AND WOULD BE TOTALLY OUT OF REACH IF COPIES WERE NOT POSSIBLE.

The visual arts have been a means of documenting great events and explaining the virtues of life throughout the ages. Great paintings tell great stories--from primitive African depictions and the ancient Egyptian world, to the riches of Greek and Roman mythology. Remarkable art always stands the test of time.

Famous paintings by the most influential artists are cost prohibitive in their original format; however, art enthusiasts and collectors can own a nearly perfect likeness—a painting recreated just for them that captures the original's beauty and splendor. For instance, a finely made copy can be painted in a size that is most suitable for a collector's home. Yes, the great paintings of the world can be available to you in a size and format that fits perfectly in whatever room you choose.

Whether you desire an impressionist painting by **Pierre-Auguste Renoir, Claude Monet,** or **Edgar Degas**, or an old-world master such as **Peter Paul Rubens, Titian,** or **Diego Velázquez**, a customized replica can be made just for you. Imagine the experience of living with such a painting and enjoying a master work over and over again. Whether you are relaxing in your favorite room or chair, in the library or at the piano, you will be constantly inspired by the presence of such greatness.

This is not a new concept. Man has reconstructed the past in one form or another since time immemorial. Extraordinary art truly enhances any mood and lifestyle. An exceptional painting is so much more than simply a decorative element. We are uplifted, sometimes even entranced, and often inspired to explore our own creativity. High-caliber artwork transports us back in time, and we feel in touch with moments, events, and feelings that occurred centuries ago.

Many of the world's great original oil paintings and exquisite copies by contemporary artists have made a political statement through subject matter and style. Certainly **Picasso**'s monumental *Guernica* movingly depicts the horrors of war, particularly the suffering it inflicts upon innocent civilians. The painting has become a universal anti-war symbol promoting the virtues of peace.

Photographer, Ray Tag / Rex USA

**GUERNICA**
*by Picasso*

At the other end of the spectrum, there are collectors who want to own a historical painting, such as *The Declaration of Independence* by **John Trumbull**, because it is so inspirational. This painting gives the American viewer, especially, an intimate sense of the birth of our nation, when the beginnings of freedom stirred as a young America broke free from England's rule. The early American statesmen shown in the painting, each one a notable and noble man, give the viewer a sense of the moral character that shaped our nation, and ultimately impacted the entire world.

DECLARATION OF INDEPENDENCE
*by Trumball, John*

War and peace are the subjects of a multitude of famous paintings. One that comes to mind is *The Execution of Emperor Maximilian* by **Edouard Manet,** painted in 1867, and currently exhibited at Stadtische Kunsthalle, Mannheim (Germany).

This painting illustrates the climax of a well-known historical event in which Napoleon III of France installed Maximilian, a member of the Hapsburg family of Austria, to power in Mexico to gain a presence there and collect unpaid debts. The plan failed and ended with the execution of Maximilian and two of his generals by firing squad by order of Benito Juárez, who had been displaced as president when the French took over. **Manet** captures the power and emotion of this significant moment.

Artistic documentation of history occurs again and again throughout the centuries, and many artists were influenced by other artists. For instance, the Manet painting we just discussed is heavily influenced by Spanish artist **Francisco Goya**'s *Third of May*, which he painted in 1808. Although it documents a totally different historical event, the painting clearly influenced **Manet**'s composition and palette. (The **Goya** now resides in the Prada Museum in Madrid.)

The world is filled with amazing works of art that have enthralled viewers of all walks of life for hundreds, even thousands, of years. For most of these fans, the only way to own a favorite masterpiece is to buy a superbly crafted copy. The key is to find a really spectacular copy that is true to the original in every way. But where do you go for such an exquisite duplicate, a masterpiece in its own right?

**THE EXECUTION OF EMPEROR MAXIMILIAN 1867**
*by Manet, Edouard*

**THIRD OF MAY 1808**
*by Goya, Francisco*

# Collecting And Enjoying Great Art Reproductions

Y OU MIGHT HAVE BEEN AMONG THE CROWD AT A MUSEUM OR GALLERY RECENTLY, STANDING IN FRONT OF A PAINTING AND GETTING GOOSE BUMPS. YOU MIGHT HAVE EVEN FELT AWE AND MARVELED AT HOW YOU COULD REACT SO STRONGLY. ONCE YOU LEFT THE MUSEUM, YOU MIGHT HAVE WONDERED HOW YOU COULD RECREATE THOSE INTENSE FEELINGS ABOUT A WORK OF ART OUTSIDE OF A MUSEUM. SOME PEOPLE ARE PASSIONATE ABOUT ART; MAYBE YOU ARE ONE OF THEM.

photographer, Graeme Harris, (Stone), Getty Images

**THE LOURVE PARIS**
Visitors Admiring Mona Lisa
*by da Vinci, Leonardo*

When you remove the obstacle of not having millions of dollars to invest in art--and you discover a reliable source for superbly painted reproductions--you realize there are endless possibilities. Why not "own" a **Monet, van Gogh, Rembrandt**, or **Degas** to enjoy in your home?

Think of what a **Raphael** would do for your home office, a painting such as *The School of Athens*, which is sure to stimulate lofty thoughts and

SCHOOL OF ATHENS
*by Raphael*

contemplation. As the owner of *Prestige Fine Art*, I have watched the eyes of countless collectors light up as we delivered a completed painting, ready to grace the wall of a special room. Rather than search for the perfect subject in the perfect size, you will get the painting of your dreams if you order an excellent copy of one that you know and love. We are not talking about prints or posters. We are talking about real paintings with sumptuous depth and texture that capture the spirit of an original—so much so that you can be sure that those goose bumps will return. A customized copy of this caliber will give you a sense of pride and admiration, and instantly elevate the tone of your surroundings.

Our clientele includes doctors who have small children and want paintings that speak to them and teach them the important lessons in life. One such doctor started his family's collection with *Daniel and the Lion's Den* by **Rubens** and went on to purchase three more paintings in a similar style. Paintings give the viewer an awareness of culture, past and present, and this doctor wanted his children to start early.

*A good painting, to me, has always been like a friend. It keeps me company, it comforts and inspires.*

*Hedy Lamar*

You do not need to look very far to realize that enhancing your environment with paintings that reflect your values and beliefs has enormous benefits.

A client once told me, "Ed, I have plenty of stocks and bonds and money in the bank. But they do not bring me the joy that I get when I look at the fine paintings on my walls."

This client was describing something we have heard over and over again for more than 20 years. Yes, it is great to have financial security, but what about how we live our lives? What we surround ourselves with provides the daily visual experiences that feed our hearts, minds, and souls. Television and posters will not achieve this, but paintings imbued with meaning and emotion—paintings that have shaped our civilization—can shape our own world and bring immeasurable joy and pleasure to our family and friends.

A successful real estate developer, and a client, told me, "The enjoyment I get when sitting in my easy chair admiring **William Bouguereau**'s *Broken Pitcher* is hard to describe. I love it, and I look forward to seeing it when I come home."

This painting is his favorite among the ten he has ordered from us (maybe because it was his first), and he hung it next to a grand piano surrounded by several chairs to relax in the moment. To an art lover, life doesn't get any better than this!

THE BROKEN PITCHER
*by Bouguereau, Adolphe William*

Alex Green, a very successful investment-advisor-turned-speaker and a *New York Times* bestselling author, relays his art experience.

He explained to his wife that the paintings in their home have to mean something to him. They have to stand for what he believes in. The first painting he purchased from *Prestige Fine Art* was **Emanuel Leutze**'s *Washington Crossing the Delaware*. Fittingly, the painting is placed

WASHINGTON CROSSING THE DELAWARE
*by Leutz , Gottlieb*

prominently over a stone fireplace at his home in Virginia. Alex also informed me that the walls of Thomas Jefferson's home in Monticello, Virginia, are enhanced by reproductions, too, including portraits of Thomas Jefferson and many others.

Remember, the art works that *Prestige Fine Art* recreates for our collectors are not prints that have been painted over, or poorly reproduced paintings whose color and technique do not match the original. Our paintings are recreated by highly skilled artists who understand the artistic nuances of the artist they are copying. These artists are honored to be commissioned to create a reproduction of a masterpiece, often painted by one of their heroes--a great artist who inspired them to become a painter in the first place.

ALEX GREEN FIREPLACE

Like you, our artists are passionate about the paintings they see at museums around the world. They take their commissions very seriously and step up to the challenge with everything they have. Whether the chosen artist works in pastel, watercolor, or oil on canvas, he or she is dedicated to amazing the collector with the finished product.

Our clients know this and give the utmost care to their reproductions, treating them as heirlooms to pass down to their children and grandchildren. One client ordered four western scenes by **Charles Russell** and asked each of his four grandchildren to select a favorite so he could add them to his will.

A longtime client from Beverly Hills used to contact us every year during his lifetime (his name was Dr. Lynn, and he lived to the ripe age of 87) to discuss which small paintings he would gift to his top accounts for the holidays. He gave generous gifts of artwork to his friends and colleagues over the years which made both him and them very happy. Dr. Lynn thought that giving paintings was a unique way to make others feel special. Plus, think of the dividends this paid him over the years; he will be forever remembered by his colleagues and art collector friends. Dr. Lynn knew this, and it brought him so much pleasure.

Imagine having someone give you a gift of the *Pathway to Giverney* by **Claude Monet**. Well, it looks like another collector has followed in Dr. Lynn's footsteps. He recently selected the **Monet** and two other paintings as gifts for his closest friends. The cycle continues.

**THE GARDEN PATH, GIVERNY**
*by Monet, Claude*

# Forgers, Artists, Copyists:  What's The Difference?

*"A true artist is characterized by an irresistible urge in the creative arts."*

*--Albert Einstein*

Forgery, as defined in *Webster's Dictionary*:  *the act or legal offense of imitating works of art to deceive.*

Forger is defined as: *one who commits forgery* (creating art intended to deceive).

Picture yourself in the National Museum of Art in Washington, DC.  The docent is walking your group through the galleries and stops in front of a great painting.  You appraise it slowly, saying that it is the greatest masterpiece you have ever seen.  You love everything about it--the composition, the palette, the painterly style.  The only word to describe the painting, you say, is "breathtaking."

The docent pauses for a few seconds, and then tells everyone, "Yes, it is very lovely, but it is not authentic."

Then you learn that the painting is actually an art forgery painted by one of the most notorious master forgers the art world has ever known, Elmyr de Hory. A few seconds ago you loved the painting. Knowing who painted it has not changed the painting, has it? If you like it less just because you know it is a fake, who is the real fraud now? This is a question that Clifford Irving (guilty of fraud in his own right; it takes one to know one), explores in his book, *Fake*, about Elmyr de Hory, who famously said that "all the great museums in America had his art and did not know it." John Connolly, former Governor of Texas, is said to have purchased 100 oil paintings by de Hory. It sounds like he has a superior collection!

photographer, Pierre Boulat, (Time & Life Pictures) Getty Images

**Henri Matisse Drawing**
Forger Elmyr de Hory

It is stories like these and many more that validate owning museum copies for enjoyment. The art of forgery is nothing new in the art world; it has gone on for centuries.

According to the book, *Fakes & Forgeries*, written by Brian Innes for *Reader's Digest* in 1997, an investigation by *The Art Newspaper*, London, alleged that at least 45 paintings and drawings attributed to the post-impressionist painter, **Vincent van Gogh** (1853-1890), which were hanging in many of the world's leading museums, were, in fact, fakes. The publication commented further that the authenticity of another 100 paintings was very much in doubt. Some of those "doubtful" paintings, such as one similar to **van Gogh**'s *Fourteen Sunflowers* (dated August 1888) in London's National Gallery were later deemed to be authentic.

**SUNFLOWERS**
*by Gogh, Vincent van*
Prestige copy

This particular sunflower painting hung in the National Gallery for ten years and was never questioned. Then doubts arose for whatever reasons, which were later quelled by the experts. Still, the fact that the painting's standing of authenticity has changed over the years, from authentic to doubtful and back to authentic, makes us wonder. How many other paintings out there have dubious or changeable authenticity? Documentation in *Fakes & Forgeries* raises doubts about so many other artworks across the spectrum, that it is beyond the scope of this writing to cover them. Bottom line: it seems that the experts are never quite settled about the authenticity of some paintings, one way or the other.

Stories about master forgers abound. Emile Schuffenecker (1851-1934) was suspected of having forged at least three paintings attributed to **van Gogh**. French forger Francis Legrange (1894-1964) won a prize in a competition for the design of a French postage stamp, but it turns out he copied another artist's work, which happened to reside in a nearby museum. In fact, his copy secretly replaced the original in that museum--so the original could be sold to an American suitor! Talk about conspiracies!

Another master forger, Eric Hebborn (1934-1996), was one of the most successful of the twentieth-century. As a student, he worked as a painting restorer, cleaning, retouching, and learning how to imitate a painting's aged, cracked look. These same techniques are utilized by *Prestige Fine Art*'s painters to create an antiquing and crackling effect upon the surface of our recreations of the old masters.

Hebborn was accepted into the Royal Academy schools where he was awarded a silver medal and a rare scholarship to study art in Italy. He became, without a doubt, a master craftsman. *The Art Forger's Handbook*, which he authored in 1997, provides extensive information about his techniques. In the book, he is quoted as saying, "There is no such thing as a fake…only fake experts and their fake labels."

**"There is no such thing as a fake…only fake experts and their fake labels."**

*Drawn to Trouble: Confessions of a Master Forger: A Memoir and*
*The Art Forgers Handbook by Eric Hebborn*

ERIC HEBBORN - 1994

Hebborn's life ended badly. He was found on a street in Rome on January 8, 1996, bludgeoned to death. He was an enemy in the eyes of some in the art world, perhaps because he was so outspoken about his work as a master forger. The murderer was never found.

Tom Keating (1917-1984) was a Londoner who pursued a successful career as an art forger. What is remarkable about Keating is that, unlike Hebborn, he did not use authentic materials. Instead he utilized synthetic materials to reproduce the works of more than 100 different artists, including **Rembrandt, Goya, Turner, van Gogh, Degas, Monet**, and **Sisley**.

**"The Fakes Progress" written by Tom Keating (1978)**

photographer, John Dee, Rex/USA

**TOM KEATING - 1977**

To compound all of the confusion between originals and forgeries, many craftsmen were also able to forge provenances (record of ownership for a work of art, ideally from the time it left the artist's studio to its present location). This additional deceit makes it even more difficult for experts to determine what is real and what has been forged from an original painting. Further complicating the situation, the forgeries where bought and sold over many years to various unsuspecting collectors, some of whom donated the works to museums and other collections. You can see how all of these circumstances can confuse even the world's top art experts.

"Forging a **Giacometti** or a **Braque** was the easy part. The genius of the con rested in faking the provenance. The art world may never know how much damage was done." This is a quote taken from an article written by Peter Landesman for *The New York Times Magazine*, July 18, 1999. The forger who said this is the 20th century master forger, John Myatt, who was also quoted as saying that "he had no idea how many millions of dollars had changed hands on account of his paintings."

In a home that was raided in London, hundreds of documents from the Victoria & Albert Museum, the Tate Gallery, and the Institute of Contemporary Art were found. Sitting on the kitchen table were two catalogues missing from the Victoria & Albert National Art Library, still in the museum bag in which they had been smuggled out the door. The master mind behind this heist was John Drew who was in cahoots with Myatt. Perhaps Drew got the idea to forge a multitude of paintings (thus the need for the stolen catalogues) when he told Myatt, "I took one of 'your' paintings to Christie's and they said it was worth $38,000." From that promising beginning, the scam unfolded, but it all ended with prison sentences for both of them.

Sometimes the real artists who created the originals or their spouses get into the act. The widows of **Modigliani** and **Chagall** were accused of selling certificates of authentication for profit, and **Salvador Dali**, near death, signed thousands of blank pieces of paper so they could be sold after his death as "authentic" lithographs (which would actually be fakes). The list of master forgers over the centuries could fill volumes, and all of the information is well-documented.

Artist is defined by *Webster* as: *A person who works in or is skilled in any of the fine arts, esp. in painting, drawing, and sculpture. A person who does anything very well with imagination and a feeling for form, effect, etc.*

Let's turn our discussion to artists. These skilled, talented, imaginative individuals come in all shapes, sizes, and personalities. Interviewing hundreds of them over the years, I have heard some interesting stories. Many are professionally trained and schooled, while others are self-taught. I have had the opportunity to go to countless artists' studios and watch them practice their craft in the warmth of their own environment. One such artist and instructor, **Sam Adoquei**, has taught in New York City for many years at the Art Students League.

On several occasions I have had the privilege of attending his classes to observe. He maintains two studios in New York City, and for many years has taught outdoor classes in Central Park. **Sam** is always a lot of fun to visit and to talk with about the artist's way of thinking. He has also started an artist colony in France where he has been embraced by the community and honored with a key to the town. **Sam** maintains an inventory of extraordinary paintings and has painted historical works, which have been displayed at the Smithsonian and other prestigious venues.

In 2010, **Sam** completed his first of two books about artists, *How Successful Artists Study*, which is packed with information for the aspiring artist. The second book, which was published a year later, is entitled *Origin of Inspiration*. This book contains seven short essays intended to get an artist's creative juices flowing.

One of **Sam's** monumental art works is destined for the history books. Titled *The Legacy of Dr. Martin Luther King Jr.*, it is full of historical content, the kind of work that we discussed in Chapter 1, which tells the tale of an event or person in history. Excellently qualified to do so, **Sam Adoquei** has shared his exceptional insight with *Prestige Fine Art* about what to look for in a skilled copy artist.

**Dr. Martin Luther King Jr. Painting**

Legacy of Dr. Martin Luther King Jr. , tritych
by Adoquei, Samuel

**Al Razza**, aka **Razza**, is an accomplished Florida-based artist who received his fine arts degree from Massachusetts College of Art and also attended Pratt Institute in New York City. An associate, confidante, and friend for more than ten years, he has displayed his art in several museums and at numerous art events. **Razza** also teaches art at the Coral Springs Museum in Florida and maintains a studio for giving private lessons to students of all ages. Although he has the skill to paint traditional works of art (he did so in his early years), **Razza**'s first love is modern abstract expressionism, and his body of work reflects that.

SHADES OF FUTURE PAST MIXED MEDIA
*by RAZZA*

photographer, Bob Bagley

As you might imagine, we have tapped his expertise for *Prestige Fine Art* in our effort to give our clients the most excellent reproductions. Over the course of many hours and cups of coffee, we have debated the credibility of fine copies and their place in the art world. **Razza** does not copy art for us on a regular basis, although, on occasion, he has completed a work of art that needed finessing. Since he works on his own originals full-time and is extremely dedicated to his work, he is not in a position to help more than occasionally. Still, **Razza** has been invaluable in giving us an artist's objective perspective on some of the paintings we might be working on for clients. For example, he points out specific techniques that the old masters used to achieve certain effects.

Professionally trained artists are taught by studying the processes and techniques of famous artists, such as **John Singer Sargent, Winslow Homer, Manet, Monet, Renoir,** and many others. These are the same techniques that go into painting a great copy, as well. **William Bouguereau** was known for his special attention to faces, hands, and feet, while **van Gogh, Monet**, and **Renoir** used thick brush work to express emotion. Professional copyists must expertly duplicate these distinguishing nuances and characteristics.

Just the other day, I told a collector that I like to test myself at museums by not looking at the plaque on the wall that names the artist--I like to guess who the old master is simply by studying the brushwork and composition. You can also test yourself by observing photos in auction catalogues and recognizing how the painting style of one artist is influenced by another's. Most of the great masters developed signature brush work that is very distinguishable, once you begin observing. As you might expect, I have developed a good eye. As new, living artists rise in the art world, I have taken note of their particular style and how it will carry them into the future archives. I have also traveled extensively throughout the United States, Paris, London, and Italy, and had numerous conversations with artists in all of these locals.

Fifteen years ago, while in the process of opening a copy gallery in Carmel, California, I was confronted by an artist who told me he was dismayed by what I was doing. He was very upset. We argued. He felt that I was cheapening his work as an original artist and not respecting his talent. I told him that all of the artists from the past had grown up copying the masters to learn their trade, and it was their high regard for the artists and their original works that inspired them to paint.

The deciding factor in our heated discussion came when I noted that the artists that *Prestige Fine Arts* employs need the money they earn from making copies to assure that they can continue painting. Many of our copy artists also paint their own originals. By the time this particular artist left the gallery, he was no longer disgruntled. In fact, we ended up shaking hands, and he thanked me for helping his fellow artists in their quest for doing the work that they love.

As an art dealer, for the most part, I sell fine copies to clients. But if a client wishes to consult me about purchasing an original painting by any of the artists I know or work with, I am happy to assist and guide them to a trusted art dealer.

In summary, artists can be a fickle, opinionated group, but their eyes always light up when I tell them I have a commission for them to copy the painting of one of the old masters. Some artists even ask to reproduce a particular painting or artist. They might say, "Ed, I love **Caravaggio**'s work and would love to copy a painting for a fine art collector who will truly enjoy it." Part of the magic for me and the artist is in knowing the joy and happiness the collector will get from owning such a painting.

Copyist: *a person who imitates or copies.*

A copyist is both an artist and a forger, although the intent is not to deceive. Some copyists do not want their identity revealed to the public because they feel that it might diminish their integrity as artists. For the most part, we at *Prestige Fine Art* never give out the contact information of our artists. Like ghost writers in the book industry, our artists suppress their identity to the greater cause of contributing their immense talents to an excellent finished product.

A copyist's work can often be more difficult than creating an original painting from scratch when you really think about it. He or she has to adhere to every nuance of the original artist's painting and perfectly capture the color, the under painting, the brushstrokes, and every single detail in the faces and gestures. Every inch of the canvas must look exactly like the original. When an artist is painting his own original, he is free to express his thoughts and feelings on the blank canvas, without any restrictions. Whether painting a landscape, floral, or a live model, the artist is free to let his imagination run wild. The composition comes from within; there is no wrong way of painting the painting.

A copyist is one who imitates, and this presents a real challenge. It is like a good chess game. For the copyist to win the game, he must plan carefully all the right moves in advance to achieve the most favorable outcome. All of the experts I have spoken to over the years agree with me on this point. For instance, they fully understand the difficulty in creating a pointillism painting such as **George Seurat**'s *Sunday Afternoon at the Le Grand Jatte*, which is on display at the Art Institute of Chicago.

**Seurat** was an artist who, for the most part, painted with small, very carefully applied dots of paint. His work is extraordinary and very difficult to reproduce.

SUNDAY AFTERNOON ON THE ISLAND OF LA GRANDE JATTE
*by Seurat, Georges*

This is also true for the painting, *Gallery With Views of Modern Rome* , by **Pannini**, quite an undertaking for even the most skilled copy virtuoso!

**GALLERY WITH VIEWS OF MODERN ROME**
by Pannini Giovanni Paolo

Another well known artist, **Antonio Canaletto**, is known for his scenes of Venice and for his scrupulous attention to detail. His painting, *Piazza San Marco*, leaves many a master artist agog. It seems impossible to duplicate.

**PIAZZA SAN MARCO LOOKING EAST**
*by Canaletto, Giovanni Antonio*

Copyists who have mastered the ability to copy this much detail are masters in their own right. They are in a select group at the top of their class. A master copyist is the same as an expert vocalist who can sing a rendition of a great songwriter or singer's work. We all enjoy hearing the songs we love, no matter who is singing them; sometimes preferring one vocalist over another, but always enjoying the song. So I ask again, Why not own a copy of a museum painting?

As we said, a copyist can transform an original painting into any size that meets a client's needs, to make it larger or smaller to fit a particular room or space in the home. Offering such customized service creates yet another hurdle for the copyist. If the canvas size is altered from the original dimensions, the copyist must reconfigure all of the proportions and perspectives within the composition so the finished painting does not alter the original in any way.

Based on my observation, the forger, the artist, and the copyist all possess a very similar set of skills, although they are used toward different ends. While the forger has deceit on his mind, the artist wants to make his individual mark on the world. The copyist, who possesses the skills of both, works with integrity, with the aim of employing and enjoying his craft and sharing a great work with an appreciative collector.

Copying art work has gone on for centuries and will continue to bring enjoyment to all of those who appreciate what goes into recreating a masterpiece and those who want to enjoy such great artwork in their homes, but could never otherwise afford it. Rather than seeing any stigma to this kind of art making, they are in awe of the talent required to create it. Many artists themselves, once they understand the full story about creating great art copies, appreciate and want to participate in this endeavor. We at *Prestige Fine Art* urge you to enjoy both original artwork and exquisite copies, whichever might be affordable to you. You are not trying to deceive anyone with your acquisitions. You just want to pursue the splendid goal of surrounding yourself with beautiful, time-honored art.

# The Extraordinary Artists Of *Prestige Fine Art*

*"The only time I feel alive is when I am painting."*

*Vincent van Gogh*

WORKING IN THE FIELD OF FINE ART REPRODUCTION FOR MORE THAN 20 YEARS, I HAVE INTERVIEWED THOUSANDS OF ARTISTS IN SEARCH OF THE BEST; THOSE WITH THE SKILL AND TALENT TO FLAWLESSLY RECREATE MASTERPIECES. IT HAS BEEN MY EXPERIENCE THAT DIFFERENT ARTISTS OFFER DIFFERENT SPECIALTIES. SOME ARE MORE KNOWLEDGEABLE OF THE SPECIFIC TECHNIQUES, BRUSH WORK, UNDER PAINTING (PREPARATION OF A CANVAS), OR GLAZING EFFECTS USED BY A PARTICULAR ARTIST. THEREFORE, WE TRY TO MATCH EACH OF OUR ARTIST'S INDIVIDUAL STRENGTHS TO THE WORK HE OR SHE IS COPYING TO ENSURE THE MOST ACCURATE AND BEAUTIFUL RESULT.

For instance, renowned American painter **John Singer Sargent**, (1856-1925), used long brushstrokes in his portrait work. If you study one of his original portraits at the Metropolitan Museum of Art in New York, you will see the numerous skills a copyist must possess to accurately replicate such a painting.

MADAME X
*by Sargent, John Singer*

**John William Turner**, an English master who lived from 1775 to 1851, worked his canvases from bottom-to-top, utilizing an under painting beneath the actual painting, as well as layers of glazing on top of it, to achieve his signature luminosity and radiance.

VENICE BRIDGE OF SIGHS
*Ron DiScenza*
Recreating Turner's painting

VENICE BRIDGE OF SIGHS
*by Turner, J.M.W.*
Tate Gallery, London, England

RON DISCENZA
Underpainting

French painter **Paul Gauguin**, (1848-1903), actually painted on burlap sacks. In order for our artists to recreate a Gauguin painting, they must begin with a roughly woven canvas so the surface replicates the kind of material that Gauguin employed.

WHERE DO WE COME FROM WHAT ARE WE WHERE ARE WE GOING
*by Gauguin, Paul*

**William Harnett**, an Irish-born American painter of the 19th century, was known for his amazing *trompe l'oeil* (literally, fool the eye) paintings of everyday objects, which achieved such astonishing verisimilitude that the viewer feels the need to reach out and touch the canvas to make sure the objects are not real.

MUSIC AND LITERATURE
*by Harnett William*

During the 15th and 16th centuries, the art of copying original artworks was strongly encouraged. Close copies of famous paintings by apprentices working in the original artists' actual studios often made distinguishing a copy from the true original almost impossible. This practice, coupled with the high demand for these great paintings, began an interesting cycle: originals and copies were comingled and passed down from generation to generation without documentation, and in some cases the copies were signed by the original old master himself!

Turner produced copies based on the work of his predecessors, including the Dutch painter **William van de Velde** (1611-1693) and French painter **Claude Lorraine** (1600-1682). The artists at *Prestige Fine Art* are aware of all of this history and truly understand what it takes and what is expected of them to create stunning reproductions for our clients.

To further heighten the scope of talent we offer at *Prestige Fine Art*, our artists come from all over the world. Here is a sampling.

## Artist from Italy

**Ron DiScenza** grew up visiting the museums of Rome as a young boy. He spent hundreds of hours viewing works by the old masters. He scrutinized the paintings and he read everything he could about the art and the artists. As he grew to understand what goes into a great work of art, he expanded his knowledge by traveling to other art capitals of the world--including London, where he got to know the Tate Gallery by heart, and New York, where the Metropolitan Museum became a second home. The process continues today; learning for an artist, learning never ends. Great artists always admire and appreciate another great artist's work, and they are determined to learn exactly how a certain painterly effect was achieved.

RON DISCENZA RECREATING FLAMING JUNE
*by Leighton, Frederick*
Museo de Arte, Ponce, Puerto Rico, USA

## Artist from Hungry

**Zohar**, Hungarian-born and a current resident of Florida, owns shelves and shelves of Sotheby's & Christie's auction catalogues; hundreds of them. After hours of conversation with him about his past commissions and the paintings he had completed for other collectors--typical of my lengthy interview process with prospective artists--I decided to hire him to paint *Lady with the Ermine* by **Leonardo da Vinci** (recently art critics have deemed this painting to be more notable, in terms of skill, than **Leonardo**'s famed *Mona Lisa*).

The original painting was done on wood panel, so **Zohar** prepared a wood panel by sanding and applying gesso (a plaster-like preparation) to create a surface that was ideal for reproducing an exact look-alike of the original. The beads in the necklace, the ermine held by the woman, and the gaze in her eyes are so exacting that we could hang it in a museum instead of the original, and it would challenge scholars, curators, and collectors to discern which painting is categorically the original.

As you can see, **Zohar** is a superior copyist, and he has gone on to paint many more commissions for us. After spending time with me, he understands my love for what we do at *Prestige Fine Art*, especially our ability to offer such high caliber work to art collectors without asking them to spend hundreds of thousands of dollars. One book on his bookshelf

in particular got my attention, titled *Secret Formulas and Techniques of the Old Masters* by Jacques Maroger. **Zohar** told me that the book contains an abundance of oil-based techniques invented and/or utilized by famous artists, including many secret formulas (for paints, mediums, varnishes, and more).

The author was the technical director of the Louvre Museum's laboratory in Paris and also served as president of the Restorers of France, among other art-related posts, so he was privy to a plethora of fascinating and invaluable information. The book is a treasure trove, indeed. I purchased a copy of my own, and many of my other artists marvel at the vital information the

THE LADY WITH THE ERMINE (CECILIA GALLERANI)
*By da Vinci, Leonardo*

book contains.

**Zohar** also painted another **Leonardo da Vinci** masterpiece, *Ginevra de' Benci*, for a lawyer in Atlanta, and a funny thing happened when I gave him the commission. **Zohar** told me, "Edward, I have done restoration work on the original at the National Gallery in Washington, D.C." It was inevitable—we produced a true masterpiece for this lucky collector!

GINERVA DE BENCI
*by da Vinci, Leonardo*

### Artist from Belgium

A close friend from Florida and a client brought an artist to my gallery to see if we had some work for him. (It is interesting that when you are in the fine art reproduction business, a lot of artists and friends of artists seek you out.) It turns out that this artist, who is from Belgium and goes only by the name of **Peter**, has a great personality to go along with his talent. He had reproduced an exact copy of an alter painting by Flemish Baroque painter **Sir Anthony Van Dyck**, (1599-1641), which is in a Belgium church. (The original and copy are both 40 feet wide!) Peter wanted to know if I would represent him in offering to sell this great reproduction to the Metropolitan Museum for millions of dollars.

Since then, he has become a valued copyist for us and has recreated several well-known Flemish floral paintings, some of the best I have ever seen.

COPY OF GHENT ALTAR
PAINTING ST BRAVO,
GHENT BY PETER
ORIGINAL
*by Jan Van Eyck*

PETER PAINTED HIS FACE IN THE COPY AS A SELF PORTRAIT,
*self portrait, VanEyckAlterPtg*

## Artist from USA

**Angel Garcia**, who lives in Florida, is our **Michelangelo** of the United States. He is another artist whose talents I have engaged many times, and he is a master painter in his own right. He possesses great range as a copyist. He has managed to capture the look of an Italian fresco from the Sistine Chapel with a plaster reproduction using colored inks, as well as an oil painting by **Degas** (one of **Angel's** favorite painters). No matter what the project, he has delivered time and time again--to the immense satisfaction of our fine art collectors.

**BASKET OF FLOWERS**
*by Bosschaert, Ambrosius*
(The Elder) Copy *by Peter*

THE DANCING CLASS BY DEGAS
*Recreated by Angel Garcia*

**ANGEL MUSICIAN 2**
*by Melozzo da Forti (fresco)*

*Angel Garcia Prestige Artist ( Michelangelo of Florida)*

## Artist from Brazil

A Brazilian-born artist from San Paulo, **Paolo Matioli** has established himself in his home town as a well-known muralist. He is self-taught and has been painting since the early age of ten. **Paolo** is a master impressionist artist capable of copying many of the famous impressionists.

He and I traveled to Washington, D.C., to visit several museums and take notes on one painting in particular, the *Luncheon of the Boating Party* by **Renoir**, which is housed at the Corcoran Gallery in the nation's capital. We had a client who wanted a perfect replica of this great work, and, as always, the project required extensive research.

At the time of our visit, there was a small sofa placed about ten feet from the painting, which was given a prominent spot in the museum. Paolo and I sat on this sofa for well over a half-hour while he used his hand-held video camera to film every square inch of the painting, including meticulous studies of the faces, hands, and shoulders of all of its subjects. (The facial expressions make it an especially joyous work.)

In this manner, **Paolo** gathered what he needed to recreate the painting in its original dimensions. Along with our other artists, **Paolo** has taught me that film, video, and photographic references are crucial to masterfully copying an old master painting. The artist who is doing the copying must be able to clearly see every single detail that must be duplicated. **Paolo** has made many of my collectors extremely happy over many years. His ability to obtain the true look and feel of a painting is always remarked upon, and this is something people speak of when they are assessing an artist's natural talents. He has the gift.

LUNCHEON OF THE BOATING PARTY
*by Renoir, Pierre Auguste*

The list of artists that we employ and continue to work with is always growing. The talent and standards that we at *Prestige Fine Art* demand--and our ability to select just the right artist to match an exclusive commission--are the key to our strength as a world-class fine art copy purveyor.

(You can read letters from satisfied collectors at the back of this book.)

Here **Paolo** creates **van Gogh's** Masterpiece "Irises". In the same manner, Paulo visited the Getty Museum where the original is located.

He took notes on the techniques and color palettes used by **van Gogh**, returned to his studio and went to work.

THE IRISES BY GOGH, VINCENT VAN
*Recreated by Paolo Matioli*
Getty Museum, Los Angeles, CA USA

# Lesser-Known Versus Famous Masterpieces

*"What I am seeking is not the real, and not the unreal, but rather the unconscious, the mystery of the instinctive in the human race ..."*

*Amedeo Modigliani*

WITH SUCH A VAST WORLD COLLECTION OF ART TO CHOOSE FROM, YOU MIGHT DECIDE TO HAVE A PAINTING RECREATED THAT IS BEAUTIFUL BUT NOT AS FAMOUS OR RECOGNIZABLE AS SOME OF THE MORE FAMILIAR GREAT WORKS. YOU MIGHT PREFER GOING IN THIS DIRECTION FOR YOUR OWN PERSONAL REASONS OR BECAUSE YOUR HOME OR OTHER SURROUNDINGS CALLS FOR A LESSER-KNOWN WORK INSTEAD. SOME COLLECTORS HAVE TOLD ME THAT THEY COULD NEVER OWN A PAINTING THAT IS SO FAMOUS THAT EVERYONE WHO VISITS WILL KNOW THAT IT IS NOT AN ORIGINAL. ONE EXAMPLE OF SUCH A LEGENDARY WORK WOULD BE THE *MONA LISA* BY **LEONARDO DA VINCI**, WHICH EVERYONE KNOWS IS HOUSED IN THE LOUVRE MUSEUM IN FRANCE. ANOTHER EXAMPLE WOULD BE *THE BAR AT THE FOLLIES BERGERE* BY **EDOUARD MANET**, WHICH IS IN THE PERMANENT COLLECTION OF THE COURTLAND INSTITUTE IN LONDON. THESE PAINTINGS BY GREAT MASTER ARTISTS ARE SO WELL-KNOWN BY THE PUBLIC THAT EVERYONE KNOWS EXACTLY WHERE THEY ARE EXHIBITED.

THE BAR AT THE FOLIES-BERGERE
*by Manet, Edouard*

PORTRAIT OF MONA LISA
*by da Vinci, Leonardo*

Some collectors are embarrassed or bothered by the concept of displaying an obvious copy of a great painting (not because the copy is not perfect, but because everyone will immediately know it is a copy, for the reasons stated above). Perhaps some collectors feel that if a viewer knows a painting is a copy, it will be less appealing to him or her. Based on my observations over many years, I respectfully disagree. In fact, many of the most resistant collectors eventually warm up to the idea of owning a great copy of a highly recognizable painting that they have always admired in a museum setting—because, in the end, they are thrilled at the prospect of enjoying such a work in the comfort of their own home.

I have also worked with collectors who do not care what other people think of their private collections. For instance, casino owner Lyle Berman had no qualms ordering *Luncheon of the Boating Party* and *Moulin de le Galette* by **Renoir**, recreated in their original sizes of approximately 5 x 6 feet. He often expresses the absolute pleasure of owning these hand-painted reproductions of masterpieces that he has always loved. He displays them in his front office to enjoy every day, along with eight other great works of art that he asked us to reproduce.

LUNCHEON OF THE BOATING PARTY
*by Renoir, Pierre Auguste*

AU MOULIN DE LA GALETTE, *by Renoir, Pierre Auguste*

Don't get me wrong; there are also merits to owning lesser-known works of art. Collectors are often inspired to have these paintings recreated in very personal dimensions, perhaps because they feel freer to do so than with a very well-known piece. As an example, I would like to point out *A Friday at the Salon of French Artist* by **Jules-Alexandre Grün**, 1868-1934.

I have yet to find any art dealers, curators, or museum directors with whom I work (and enjoy intense discussions about art) who can immediately identify this artist or the location of his original paintings! This particular painting is similar in composition to the earlier referenced *Moulin de le Galette* by **Renoir** (perhaps an influence), yet the viewer does not recognize it to be a famous impressionist painting by a famous impressionist artist, although it is exquisite in its mood and detail.

**A FRIDAY AT THE SALON OF THE FRENCH ARTISTS**
*by Grun, Jules Alexandre*

In similar fashion, a prolific American artist named **Edward Potthast**, 1857-1927, known for his atmospheric New York and New England beach scenes, and who never attained the notoriety of other American impressionists (although his work is included in many major museums in the United States), can be exhibited in your home without anyone ever knowing that it is a reproduction.

Because **Potthast** is reasonably priced at auction ($25 thousand to $100 thousand), fine art collectors often own multiples, also possible because **Potthast** left a large body of work (his original paintings number into the hundreds). His works are owned by many different private collectors, so even to the art aficionado who visits a painting-filled home for a party or event, a good reproduction of his work would most likely be taken for an original.

**MANHATTAN BEACH**
*by Potthast, Edward Henry*

**CHILDREN ON THE BEACH**
*by Potthast, Edward Henry*

**THE BUCKET BRIGADE**
*by Potthast, Edward Henry*

**CHILDREN AT SHORE NO. 3**
*by Potthast, Edward Henry*

**BRIGHTON BEACH**
*by Potthast, Edward Henry*

On several occasions collectors I work with tell me, "Ed, I do not want anything that is easily recognizable as a reproduction. Can you locate an artwork that is in a private collection or a painting that I could be perceived to feasibly own (say, the original is priced under $100,000) as an anonymous collector?" For this type of client, I search the Sotheby's and Christie's auction catalogues to find just the right artwork to match these exacting requirements. The art world contains a multitude of superior art works by lesser-known artists, which can be enjoyed without worry or concern that they will be spotted as copies and not originals—especially if they are shown next to other original paintings as part of a complete collection.

Then again, on other occasions, I hear this from my collectors: "I need to find fine art reproductions that will work well with the originals in my existing collection. These paintings would be for my second home, and I do not want to spend a fortune on the paintings or the insurance for a home that I rarely live in. What's more, I need specific sizes for different areas in this home--over the fireplace, niches in paneled areas, over the headboards in the bedrooms, smaller bathroom spaces, and entrance ways." The list goes on and on.

The beauty of *Prestige Fine Art* is that we can accommodate all of these very specific requests to the letter. Whatever your philosophy about lesser-known versus well-known works of art might be; wherever you might need your reproduced paintings to fit—within an existing art collection, standing alone, or created especially for a separate house or unique environment—we can satisfy your every need, desire, wish, or whim--in a way that our experience tells us will make you very happy.

# Museum Quality Framing

Framing at *Prestige Fine Art* has become an art in and of itself, and this is as it should be. Our philosophy about framing is that the frame should compliment the painting and not distract from it in any way. There is a marriage between frame and painting that, when done correctly, adds a final, beautiful touch. When someone is viewing a painting, his or her eyes should never dart back-and-forth from painting to frame. This is annoying and takes away from the viewer's pleasure. Ideally, the eyes should rest easily upon a work of art to savor its splendor, appreciate what the artist has accomplished, and indulge in the painting's beauty—freeing the mind to ponder its meaning. The frame should enhance these visual experiences in the best way possible and show off the painting at its best.

In short, proper framing is very important. I have visited so many museums and at times thought the paintings were either under- or over-framed, diminishing my enjoyment of the exhibition. There are several reasons for such framing miscalculations, but one stands out: museums must sometimes reframe a piece for whatever reason, and somebody unqualified on the museum staff does the job without knowing how to properly do it. I have even observed poor framing at one of the top museums in New York! During one visit, I noticed that something was just "not right" with a particular painting and later learned, either after reading the show's accompanying literature or being told by a staff member, that the frame I was looking at was not the original frame chosen by the artist. Of course--the artist would have never chosen a poor frame.

Earlier in my career I visited museums around the United States and Europe to photograph the original paintings that my artists planned to copy, including the frames. By doing this, I felt I would be better able to place our copies of famous paintings into frames similar to, or the same as, those the original artist had selected. This process also gave me the education necessary to talk to collectors in a knowledgeable manner. Whenever any of those collectors wished to view the original framing of a particular painting, I was prepared. I kept a large photograph album of the paintings in their frames, with a notation of the museums in which they were located. To this day, I continue to maintain the album.

I have had many conversations with museum framers in the U.S., such as Eli Wilner, Lowy, Regence, and Munn. These are the very same framing houses that assist collectors who purchase famous original paintings, by artists such as **Monet, Rembrandt**, or **van Gogh**, etcetera. Museums often also assist in the framing of great masterpieces that have been purchased by individual collectors. In our relentless quest for authenticity, *Prestige Fine Art* uses these notable framers for our copies of fine works of art. Why not frame our reproductions in the very best frames, those that were best suited to the originals? The result is framing that adds the perfect finishing touch to a painting, maximizing the viewer's enjoyment and creating an exhilarating experience equal to visiting a great museum or seeing a wonderful art show in a gallery.

THE AMBASSADORS
*by Holbein, Hans*

Another way to incorporate museum frames into your art collection is to find an antique frame and commission a reproduction of the classical painting of your choice--to be created just for that frame. I have traveled to France and bid on whole collections of old frames in small countryside towns just for this purpose. The antique dealers I met knew the sources of the frames they carried, which were often found in old buildings and farm houses where they had been stored for years. Some of these frames have unique carvings intended to enhance master works. The only caveat or downside: you must be careful in handling these sometimes fragile frames and make sure they have been inspected for dry rot or bugs. I have also seen entire second-floor flats in Manhattan lined with hundreds of old frames—stored there for the purpose of selling them to someone who wants to build a painting around a particular frame.

Still another source for old frames is your local auction house. They buy complete estates that might include old paintings and frames that are still in good shape. Many of these frames are of a caliber that warrants having a painting made for them (fitted to the frame's exact dimensions), or, as we say, "painted in the exact size to fit the frame." We have also restored some of these old frames to give a painting the look of a true old-world masterpiece.

PAINTER'S SALON
*by Stevens, Alfred*

Curating old frames is a thriving business. Eli Wilner and Lowy specialize in selling collectible frames, which can range in price from $5,000 to well over $35,000. These frames are cherished for their own beauty, separate from a painting's.

As we said in an earlier chapter, one unique aspect of making copies of great paintings is that the buyer can pre-select the painting size and have it customized to meet particular needs or preferences. This flexibility opens up a whole world of possibilities for creating custom paintings in a style that compliments an existing, often much-treasured, heirloom or antique frame.

*Prestige Fine Art* has actually had the experience of dealing with an owner of an original painting (specifically *Portrait of a Man* by **Bronzino**) who had to sell the work at auction but kept the frame--and asked us to paint a reproduction of the original painting, intended specially for the original frame. This particular painting had been in the collector's family for years, and he very much wanted to keep its "energy" in the family. He even flew our artist to the location of the original painting, where the artist took notes and made color matches in order to create a copy that was as close to the original as possible. His groundwork even included preparing a panel of wood exactly like the original was painted upon. You can imagine; the final reproduction was quite a masterpiece.

Framing is the final touch to the artist's craft and, therefore, an integral part of our craft. We have ample frame resources to assure our art collectors total satisfaction no matter what their budget. The *Prestige Fine Art* frame shop is equipped to assemble frames from lengths of ten-foot moldings, and we can add linen liners, gold lips, and filets. We offer hand-carved 24kt gold leaf frames with finishes that can be fine-tuned to achieve the exact look you desire—creating that ideal marriage of painting and frame. The choices are unlimited.

# World Class Museums

MUSEUMS ARE THE GREAT GATE KEEPERS OF THE WORLD'S MASTERPIECES OF ART. ONLY MUSEUMS CAN GATHER A SELECTION OF HUMANITY'S GREATEST PAINTINGS, SCULPTURES, PHOTOGRAPHS, AND ART OBJECTS UNDER ONE ROOF. MUSEUMS ENABLE ART ENTHUSIASTS TO SHARE THE SAME ROOM WITH BELOVED MASTERPIECES FOR A MOMENT IN TIME. IN MY EARLY YEARS AS AN ART DEALER SELLING FINE ART COPIES, I TOOK ADVANTAGE OF THE SPECIAL OPPORTUNITIES THAT VISITING MUSEUMS AFFORDED, AND I TRAVELED TO AS MANY AS MY TIME AND BUDGET WOULD ALLOW. THIS GAVE ME A SOLID FOUNDATION ON THE SUBJECT OF THE OLD MASTERS' STYLES AND TECHNIQUES, ESPECIALLY THOSE THAT WERE MOST IN DEMAND BY MY CLIENTS AND COLLECTORS. I WOULD GET UP VERY CLOSE TO STUDY VAN GOGH'S *STARRY NIGHT* AT THE MUSEUM OF MODERN ART IN NEW YORK CITY OR HIS FAMED *IRISES* AT THE GETTY MUSEUM IN CALIFORNIA, A $50 MILLION ACQUISITION BY THAT MUSEUM BACK IN 1980.

**STARRY NIGHT**
*by Gogh, Vincent van*
Museum of Modern Art, NYC, USA

I was surprised and pleased that while visiting the Getty I was allowed to photograph **van Gogh**'s *Irises*, which I later utilized to great effect at a speaking engagement for a well-known Dale Carnegie organization. During my talk, I placed a copy of the painting done by *Prestige Fine Art* on an easel next to my photograph of the original in the museum, which was blown up to the painting's actual size.

IRISES
*by Gogh, Vincent van*
The Getty Museum, Los Angeles, CA USA

Using this visual aid, I was able to not only explain to the audience just how accurate our copy of the masterpiece was, but I was able to show them, detail by detail. This brought home the point I was making: why would a worldly and famous investment advisor, author, and speaker, Mr. Mark Skousen, purchase the copy as a gift for his mother who loved the Dutch master's *Irises*? The answer was plain to see. Skousen was able to make his mother feel like she was living with the treasured original masterpiece and really could not tell the difference. What a gift of joy her son was able to give her! My Dale Carnegie audience was also captivated, and they marveled at the exact likeness demonstrated through my detailed comparison.

At about the time that the Japanese and the Getty where bidding to purchase *Irises*, I had a rather unique experience. I was working in my gallery office when a telephone call came in. I answered, and the voice on the other end asked for directions to the gallery, which I provided, and then I asked who was coming to visit. The caller cut me short abruptly and said, "No names, we just need directions." About 20 minutes later a limousine pulled up and two large men in dark suits walked into our spacious gallery, where hundreds of copies of famous paintings were on display.

Our anonymous guests wandered through the gallery for a couple of minutes until a third man appeared. I walked up to greet this gentleman whose hand lunged out toward mine to grasp it in a firm handshake. "Hi, I am Ross Perot," he said casually, and one of my entrepreneurial heroes was suddenly standing right in front of me.

"Where are the *Irises*?" he asked, as he looked around marveling at all the great art on the walls. He was really enjoying himself. Perot went on to explain that he was interested in purchasing this painting to play a prank on his wife, to make her think he had purchased the real thing for millions of dollars. He was also interested in *Washington Crossing the Delaware* by **Emanuel Leutz**, which is in the Metropolitan Museum of Art and one of Perot's all-time favorite paintings, so he told me. He left the gallery as quickly as he had arrived, and sometime later he purchased both paintings from me. It is always nice to meet someone in person whom you have admired since college, especially an inspiring entrepreneur.

The *Irises* brought us even more attention when we used the reproduction in a national advertising campaign. I received an official letter from the Getty Museum requesting that I discontinue using "their" painting in our advertising. I promptly wrote back, first thanking them for the wonderful compliment, and second to tell them that the painting that appeared in our ad was actually a copy of **van Gogh**'s *Irises* painted by one of our very talented artists—and we were acting totally within our legal limits because the original painting is in the public domain. I never heard another word from the Getty Museum about our advertisement.

Museums come in all shapes and sizes. Some are housed in the homes of art collectors, converted into intimate public spaces to show off and share their collections. One of the collectors I have worked with for more than ten years decided, in 2010, that she would like to have several paintings that she had admired at the Tate Gallery in London copied by a *Prestige Fine Art* artist for her own personal enjoyment. During our discussion about doing this, she exclaimed, "Edward, I can't imagine an artist being able to copy **Samuel Palmers'** *Waterfall* without actually seeing the original!"

She promptly offered to fly me from the U.S., and my artist from Italy, to England to view several **Constable**, a **Turner**, and the **Samuel Palmer** paintings she wanted copied. She told me that she and her husband visit England often and always visit the great museums. She has developed many favorite paintings, which she would love to own to capture her memories of their visits to such wonderful monuments to art. Then she realized that *Prestige Fine Art* could make this dream a reality.

Of course, I jumped at the opportunity. While in London, I walked to the Wallace Collection, a free museum with many fine masterpiece paintings. You can go early and have the museum all to yourself to enjoy. I was also able to visit the astute Royal Academy of Art and artist **Lord Fredrick Leighton**'s home, which, like so many other successful artists' homes, had been turned into a museum dedicated to his works of art. The National Gallery in London is another museum not to be missed. My only regret is that I often do not have enough time to spend in foreign countries to thoroughly visit all of their state and private museums, home to such beautiful treasures.

**Thanks dearly to Mrs. Jean Angle, Wichita Kansas**

On my last trip to Paris, France, I promised myself that I would return and rent a flat for at least one month to go back to the Musée de Louvre and the Musée d'Orsay and spend a few leisurely hours at a time basking in the masterpieces by my favorite artists there. Visiting museums can be an overwhelming experience. One can easily succumb to "art overload"—a tremendous overpowering of the senses. For this reason, I suggest taking your time and enjoying the artworks in small portions, without over tiring yourself or trying to cram too much seeing into too little time. In most cases, every world-class museum features several artists or art works that are on almost every art connoisseur's must-see list. At the Louvre, it's the *Mona Lisa* by **Leonardo da Vinci**. At the Tate, it is artist **William Turner**, and at the Getty, it is the famous *Irises*. Still, the list of must-see paintings might be different for some people, depending on each individual's particular tastes and preferences. Artists whom I have worked with also have favorite paintings by past masters, and they marvel at seeing their styles and techniques at various museums, up close and personal.

Often, the museums themselves are stellar works of art. The Getty Museum in California has transformed its art collections with the times, yet its fountains and architecture remain constant and are nectar for the eyes and senses. Who isn't moved when visiting the gardens and statues that line the colonnade and the long pool of the Getty Villa? When visiting New York City, art lovers gravitate to the Metropolitan Museum, the Museum of Modern Art, and the Guggenheim, but they can also find smaller, more intimate museum settings nearby. The Frick Collection, which is only blocks away from the Metropolitan Museum, is housed in a building with intricate moldings and inlays that are exquisite and worth the visit alone. What a site to see and enjoy. In fact two paintings that where viewed at the Frick by one of our New York collectors and then commissioned are shown below. The paintings are titled *Cloud Study 1 & 2 by* **John Constable**. It is being able to make the wishes of ardent art collectors come true, as we did in this case and so many others too numerous to count, that makes my own work a passion.

CLOUD STUDY 1
*by John Constable*

CLOUD STUDY 2
*by John Constable*

In true freedom style, the Philadelphia Museum of Art makes its presence known as a monument of great artistic merit that is dedicated to grand art inside. This Museum and The Barnes Collection make Philadelphia, an historic beacon of American liberty, a not-to-be-missed destination for museum and art lovers. Chicago cannot go unnoticed with its famed Chicago Art Institute, housing jewels of the art world such as **Georges-Pierre Seurat**, **Pierre-Auguste Renoir**, and **Edgar Degas** whose gorgeous works are safely tucked inside behind the museum's signature lions, guarding a treasure trove of mankind's creativity. The National Gallery in Washington, D.C., is one of several museums in the nation's capital that both houses famed art and is a masterpiece in its own right. The nearby Smithsonian and the Portrait Galleries are both easily worth several days of exploration. Take your time, and enjoy each and every moment.

Savor, too, the following pages dedicated to notable museums around the world. We have highlighted each of their distinguishing characteristics. For instance, some were designed by renowned architects, others have illustrious histories. Still others are well-known because of their size or location, or because the museum is celebrated for a particular and acclaimed work of art or artist.

# The Metropolitan Museum Of Art, New York City

A FIFTH AVENUE LANDMARK, THE "MET" IS A VIRTUAL PALACE OF ART. THE BUILDING'S GRAND, SWEEPING STAIRCASE AND BEAUX-ARTS FAÇADE ARE KNOWN THE WORLD OVER, AND THE AWE-INSPIRING BREADTH OF THE MUSEUM'S COLLECTIONS--FROM WINGS DEDICATED TO GREAT PAINTINGS AND SCULPTURE THROUGHOUT ART HISTORY, TO RARE ANTIQUITIES FROM THE EGYPTIAN, GREEK, AND ROMAN EMPIRES--IS LEGENDARY.

The Great Hall is the setting for galas and fundraisers, which draw celebrities and pillars of the arts, music, and fashion communities. Renowned blockbuster exhibitions reflect the gargantuan reach of the museum's curatorial departments.

On any given day, visitors to New York's most popular single-site tourist attraction, situated next to Central Park, flock to see their most beloved works of art--**Renoir**'s *Young Girls at the Piano*, **Pablo Picasso**'s *Portrait of Gertrude Stein*, and **Caravaggio**'s *Denial of Saint Peter*, to name a few. Following are more of the Met's signature paintings, whose reproductions are also in high demand at *Prestige Fine Art*.

photographer, Siegfried Layda, (Photographer's Choice) Getty Images

**THE METROPOLITAN MUSEUM**
*New York City, NY USA*

**THE HORSE FAIR**

*by Bonheur, Rosa*

**YOUNG GIRLS AT THE PIANO**

*by Renoir, Pierre Auguste*

**IN THE MEADOW**

*by Renoir, Pierre Auguste*

**SPRING**

*by Cot, Pierre Auguste*

**YOUNG WOMAN WITH A WATER JUG**

*by Vermeer, Jan*

**THE ARTIST'S GARDEN, VERSAILLES**

*by Manet, Edouard*

**LANDSCAPE THE PARC MONCEAU**

*by Monet, Claude*

**RECLINING NUDE**

*by Modigliani, Amedeo*

**PYGMALION AND GALATEA**

*by Gerome, Jean-Leon*

**THE GRAND CANAL, VENICE**

*by Turner, J.M.W.*

**GARDEN AT SAINTE-ADRESSE**

*by Monet, Claude*

**TOILETTE OF VENUS**

*by Boucher, Francois*

**THE STORM**

*by Cot, Pierre Auguste*

# The Louvre, Paris, France

**T**HE LOUVRE IS ONE OF THE WORLD'S LARGEST MUSEUMS, AND IT IS TRULY A MONUMENT TO ART. ITS ARCHITECTURE AND INTERIOR SPACES ARE AS RENOWNED AS ITS ART COLLECTIONS, WHICH ENCOMPASS EVERY ASPECT OF WESTERN ART. THE BUILDING HAS EVOLVED OVER 800 YEARS AND OFFERS A CONCISE HISTORY OF FRENCH ARCHITECTURE.

It began as a medieval fortress in the 12th century during the Crusades, and was later transformed, in part, into a neoclassical museum for the people, before it was expanded into a stylistically eclectic museum under Napoleon III. Most recently, over a span of about 20 years, it has been remodeled to become a state-of-the-art museum and cultural center. The famous and controversial glass pyramid at the main entrance was the beginning of this makeover and is now recognizable the world over, punctuating the contemporary aspect of this 21st century Parisian art hub.

The great works inside are equally monumental. Perhaps one painting and one sculpture are most synonymous with the Louvre: *Mona Lisa* by **Leonardo da Vinci** and *Venus Di Milo*, added to the museum's collection during the reign of Louis XVIII. There are, of course, other wildly popular works in the museum's vast rooms and hallways, and here are some of the highlights. Several of these masterpieces have been beautifully recreated by *Prestige Fine Art* for discerning collectors seeking the finest museum copies.

photographer, Scott E. Barbour (The Image Bank) Getty Images

**THE LOUVRE MUSEUM**
*Paris, France*

**GRANDE ODALISQUE**

*by Ingres, Jean-Auguste Dominique*

**PORTRAIT OF A NEGRESS, SALON OF 1800**

*by Benoist, Marie-Guillemine*

**WOMEN OF ALGIERS IN THEIR APARTMENT**

*by Delacroix, Eugene*

**THE BOLT**

*by Jean-Honore Fragonard*

**PORTRAIT OF A MAN**

*by Antonello da Messina*

**PORTRAIT OF MONA LISA**

*by da Vinci, Leonardo*

**THE ASTRONOMER**

*by Vermeer, Jan*

**THE FIFER**

*by Manet, Edouard*

**WILD POPPIES**

*by Monet, Claude*

**THE MONEY LENDER AND HIS WIFE**
*by Metsys, Quentin*

**THE CORONATION OF NAPOLEON AND JOSEPHINE**
*by David, Jacques-Louis*

**OFFICER OF THE IMPERIAL GUARD**
*by Theodore Gericault*

**THE BROKEN PITCHER**
*by Greuze, Jean Baptise*

# The National Gallery of Art, Washington, D.C.

LOCATED ON THE NATIONAL MALL OF THE NATION'S CAPITAL, THIS MUSEUM WAS FOUNDED IN 1937 FOR "WE, THE PEOPLE." THE ORIGINAL WEST BUILDING, WITH ITS STATELY COLUMNS AND DOMED ROTUNDA (MODELED ON ROME'S PANTHEON) BEFITS NEARBY CAPITOL HILL--NOT SURPRISING SINCE THE NEOCLASSICAL BUILDING WAS DESIGNED BY ARCHITECT JOHN RUSSELL POPE, WHO LATER CREATED THE JEFFERSON MEMORIAL. THE COLLECTION INCLUDES PAINTINGS, DRAWINGS, PHOTOGRAPHS, AND SCULPTURE TRACING WESTERN ART FROM THE MIDDLE AGES TO TODAY. THIS BUILDING HOUSES THE ONLY PAINTING BY **LEONARDO DA VINCI** IN THE UNITED STATES, A PORTRAIT TITLED *GINEVRA DE' BENCI*.

The modern looking East building, designed by I.M. Pei, focuses on modern art and contains a large research facility, the Center for Advanced Study in the Visual Arts. This building is also home to **Alexander Calder's** largest mobile, along with works by **Henri Matisse**, **Joan Miró**, **Pablo Picasso**, and **Jackson Pollock**. The museum's outdoor sculpture garden features modern and contemporary works.

Paintings that are viewer magnets include *Breezing Up (A Fair Wind)* by **Winslow Homer** and *Woman With A Parasol* by **Claude Monet**. Here are a few more museum and *Prestige Fine Art* favorites.

photographer, Scott E. Barbour (The Image Bank) Getty Images

**THE NATIONAL GALLERY OF ART**
*Washington DC, USA*

**BREEZING UP (A FAIR WIND)**

*by Homer, Winslow*

**THE ARTIST'S GARDEN AT VETHEUIL**

*by Monet, Claude*

**BOUQUET OF FLOWERS IN A GLASS VASE**

*by Bosschaert, Ambrosius (The Elder)*

**THE RETURN OF THE PRODIGAL SON**

*by Rembrandt, Harmensz, van Rijn*

**THE GIRL WITH A RED HAT**

*by Vermeer, Jan*

**THE BRIDGE AT ARGENTEUIL**

*by Monet, Claude*

**THE OLD VIOLIN**

*by Harnett, William Michael*

**OARSMEN AT CHATOU**

*by Renoir, Pierre Auguste*

**CATTLEYA ORCHID AND THREE BRAZILIAN HUMMINGBIRDS**

*by Heade, Martin Johnson*

**A SUMMER'S DAY**
*by Morisot, Berthe*

**THE JAPANESE FOOTBRIDGE**
*by Monet, Claude*

**HIDE AND SEEK**

by *Tissot, James Jacques Joseph*

**WOMAN WITH A PARASOL MADAME MONET AND HER SON**

by *Monet, Claude*

# The Philadelphia Museum Of Art

ALTHOUGH IT IS ONE OF THE LARGEST MUSEUMS IN THE UNITED STATES, WITH WORLD-CLASS MASTER WORKS BY SOME OF THE GREATEST AMERICAN AND EUROPEAN ARTISTS THAT EVER LIVED, INCLUDING FRENCH IMPRESSIONISTS AND POST-IMPRESSIONISTS, AND AN ALMOST UNRIVALED COLLECTION OF ASIAN ART, IT IS THE MUSEUM'S STEPS THAT HAVE BECOME A CULTURAL ICON--THE STAIRCASE THAT ROCKY BALBOA RAN UP AND DOWN TO GET INTO SHAPE. THE FILM HERO'S BRONZE STATUE STRIKES A TRIUMPHANT POSE NEARBY.

That said, the museum contains so many art objects that it would take days to see all of them, and that's before it was expanded in 2008! To help set priorities, the painting collection highlights include **Vincent van Gogh**'s *Vase With Twelve Sunflowers, Arles*, **Paul Cézanne**'s *The Bathers*, **Marcel Duchamp**'s *Nude Descending A Staircase, No. 2*, **El Greco**'s *Pietà*, and **Claude Monet**'s *Poplars, Autumn*.

The very much admired paintings below from the museum's permanent collection represent several of the museum-quality copies that *Prestige Fine Art* has produced over the years.

**THE PHILADELPHIA MUSEUM OF ART**
*Philadelphia, PA USA*
Photo includes the old waterworks building in lower front.

**BACCHUS AND ARIADNE ON THE ISLE OF NAXOS**
*by Coypel, Antoine*

**THE BATHERS**
*by Renoir, Pierre Auguste*

**ANTIBES MORNING**
*by Monet, Claude*

**MONT SAINTE-VICTOIRE**
*by Cezanne, Paul*

**THE MANTE FAMILY**
*by Degas, Edgar*

**MOTHER PROTECTING CHILD**
*by Corot, (Jean-Baptiste) Camille*

**ABDUCTION OF EUROPA**
*by Coypel, Noel-Nicolas, (extended)*

**ABDUCTION OF EUROPA**
*by Coypel, Noel-Nicolas, (detail)*

# The Art Institute of Chicago

THE LION STATUES FLANKING THE ART INSTITUTE'S MAIN ENTRANCE ON SOUTH MICHIGAN AVENUE ARE IMMEDIATELY RECOGNIZABLE, AS IS THE LARGE CANVAS UPON ENTERING: **GEORGES-PIERRE SEURAT**'S *SUNDAY AFTERNOON ON THE ISLAND OF LA GRANDE JATTE*—AS WELL AS **GUSTAVE CAILLEBOTTE**'S EQUALLY GRAND *PARIS STREET, RAINY DAY*. THIS IS ONE OF THE WORLD'S MOST WELL-KNOWN MUSEUMS, AND IT IS AMERICA'S SECOND-LARGEST, BEHIND ONLY THE METROPOLITAN MUSEUM OF ART. IT GREW FROM A SMALL DESIGN STUDIO ON DEARBORN STREET FOUNDED BY 35 ARTISTS, WITH A MISSION OF BECOMING AN ART SCHOOL AND GALLERY, TO AN ACADEMY OF FINE ARTS AFTER THE GREAT CHICAGO FIRE IN 1871. A LITTLE MORE THAN TEN YEARS AFTERWARD, IT TOOK THE NAME THAT WE KNOW TODAY AND EVENTUALLY SETTLED AT ITS PRESENT LOCATION.

In addition to the renowned paintings mentioned above, other works from the museum's collection are also some of the art world's most-celebrated (and recognizable), attracting art lovers from around the globe. These include *American Gothic* by **Grant Wood**, *Nighthawks* by **Edward Hopper**, *The Child's Bath* by **Mary Cassatt**, *The Old Guitarist* by **Pablo Picasso**, and more. Since so many of the paintings that follow are so well-known, *Prestige Fine Art* has had the privilege of creating copies of all of them.

**THE CHICAGO ART INSTITUTE**
*Chicago, Ill USA*

**SUNDAY AFTERNOON ON THE ISLAND OF LA GRANDE JATTE**
*by Seurat, Georges*

**ON THE TERRACE**
*by Renoir, Pierre Auguste*

**A HOLIDAY**
*by Potthast, Edward Henry*

**MARSEILLES, SEEN FROM L' ESTAQUE**
*by Cezanne, Paul*

**WOMAN AT HER TOILETT**
*by Morisot, Berthe*

**ODALISQUE**

*by Lefebvre, Jules Joseph*

**PARIS STREET, RAINY DAY**

*by Caillebotte, Gustave*

**THE SONG OF THE LARK**

*by Breton, Jules Adolphe Aime Louis*

**BULLFIGHT IN SPAIN**

*by Manet, Edouard*

**BRIDGE OVER WATERLILLIE POND**
*by Monet, Claude*

**WATER LILIES, 1906**
*by Monet, Claude*

# The Frick Collection

THE FRICK MANSION'S INTERIOR IS ONE OF THOSE INTIMATE GALLERY SPACES THAT RIVAL THE ARTWORK ON DISPLAY. THE GEM-LIKE ROOMS ALONE DEMAND SEVERAL UNHURRIED VISITS. AND THE ARTWORK IS SPECTACULAR. THE GOOGLE ART PROJECT (AN ONLINE ARCHIVE OF MUSEUMS AROUND THE WORLD) INCLUDES THE COLLECTION AMONG ITS VIRTUAL TOURS, PROVIDING CLOSE-UP AND DETAILED VISUAL ACCESS. SEVERAL OF THE FRICK PAINTINGS FEATURED HAVE BEEN MASTERFULLY REPRODUCED BY *PRESTIGE FINE ART*.

Located on Manhattan's Upper East Side, the Frick is the elegant backdrop to seasonal events, annual benefits, and concerts. It is also the permanent residence of some of the best-known paintings by the greatest European artists, as well as other major works of art, many acquired and donated by Henry Clay Frick when he was alive.

The breathtaking range of art is clear: **Giovanni Bellini**'s *St. Francis in the Desert,* **James Whistler's** *Portrait of Mrs. Frances Layland,* **Johannes Vermeer**'s *Officer and Laughing Girl,* **Diego Velázquez**'s *King Philip IV of Spain,* **Rembrandt**'s *Portrait of a Young Artist,* and so on. More samples follow.

photographer, Neilson Barnard (Getty Images Entertainment) Getty Images

**THE FRICK COLLECTION**
*New York City, NY USA*

Autumn Dinner (interior of the Frick utilized to enhance events)

**SELF-PORTRAIT**

*by Rembrandt Harmensz, van Rijn*

**LODOVICO CAPPONI**

*by Bronzino, Agnolo*

**COMTESSE D'HAUSSONVILLE**

*by Ingres, Jean-Auguste Dominique*

**GIRL INTERRUPTED AT HER MUSIC**
*by Vermeer, Jan*

**THE WHITE HORSE**
*by Constable, John*

**THE LOVE LETTERS**
*by Fragonard, Jean-Honore*

**THE LOVER CROWNED**
*by Fragonard, Jean-Honore*

**THE PURSUIT**

*by Fragonard, Jean-Honore*

**THE RENDEZVOUS**

*by Fragonard, Jean-Honore*

**SPRING**

*by Boucher, Francois*

**SUMMER**

*by Boucher, Francois*

**WINTER**

*by Boucher, Francois*

**THE FLUTE PLAYER**

*by Boucher, Francois*

**AUTUMN**

*by Boucher, Francois*

# The Tate Gallery

THE TATE GALLERY IS A WORK IN PROGRESS. ALTHOUGH IT BEGAN AS ONE BUILDING ON ONE SITE, THE TATE IS NOW A NETWORK OF FOUR MAJOR MUSEUMS THROUGHOUT ENGLAND, AND IT IS EXPANDING. THE CONGLOMERATE HOUSES THE UNITED KINGDOM'S NATIONAL COLLECTION OF ART FROM THE 16TH CENTURY TO THE PRESENT DAY, ALONG WITH MODERN AND CONTEMPORARY ART FROM OTHER COUNTRIES.

Before it became the Tate, the museum was called the National Gallery of British Art, seeded by a private art collection in 1847. Much later, sugar magnate Henry Tate helped fund the building of the gallery and donated his own, mostly Victorian, art collection. By 1954, the Tate was its own entity. As the collections grew over the years, the overflow spilled into separate locations.

The stars of the museum are the earlier paintings, particularly those by **Joseph William Turner**, such as *Shields, On the River Tyne*. **William Blake**'s *Nebuchadnezzar*, **John Singer Sargent**'s *Claude Monet Painting by the Edge of a Wood*, and **Johann Henry Fuseli**'s *Lady Macbeth with the Daggers* are popular draws. *Prestige Fine Art*, too, has focused on the traditional paintings, such as those below, due to our customers' wishes.

photographer, Johnnie Pakington (Digital Vision) Getty Images

**THE TATE GALLERY**
*London, England*

**MARES AND FOALS IN A RIVER LANDSCAPE**
*by Stubbs, George*

**THE GLEBE FARM**
*by Constable, John*

**THE LAMENT FOR ICARUS**
*by Draper, Herbert*

**THE GLEANING FIELD**
*by Palmer, Samuel*

**A FAVOURITE CUSTOM**
*by Alma-Tadema, Sir Lawrence*

**CARNATION LILY, LILY ROSE**
*by Sargent, John Singer*

**BRIDGE OF SIGHS**
*by Turner, William*

**THE WATERFALLS, PISTIL MAWDDUCH, NORTH WALES**
*by Palmer, Samuel*

**THE GROVE HAMPSTEAD**
*by Constable, John*

**A HILLY SCENE**
*by Palmer, Samuel*

**THE COURTYARD OF THE HOUSE OF COPTIC**

*by Lewis, John Federick*

**VENICE, BRIDGE OF SIGH**

*by Turner, William*

# The Barnes Collection

IN NEW QUARTERS IN DOWNTOWN PHILADELPHIA, ALBERT C. BARNES' COLLECTION REMAINS AN EXTRAORDINARY REPRESENTATION OF IMPRESSIONIST AND EARLY MODERNIST EUROPEAN AND AMERICAN PAINTINGS, AS WELL AS AFRICAN SCULPTURES AND PENNSYLVANIA FOLK ART. THE ROOMS REMAIN TRUE TO THE ORIGINAL SUBURBAN MERION, PENNSYLVANIA, LOCATION, AND THE ART IS DISPLAYED IN THE UNIQUE BARNES STYLE—CONTAINING DOUBLE- AND TRIPLE-HUNG WALLS, AND A POWERFUL MIX OF IMPRESSIONIST STYLES. MORE IMPORTANT, **MATISSE**, **CÉZANNE**, AND **VAN GOGH** STILL RULE.

The paintings to see are from **Matisse**'s Fauve period, namely *The Joy of Life* and *The Dance* triptych, one of the artist's renowned and colorful dance murals. For *Prestige Fine Art,* the paintings from the Barnes *collection* that we have recreated are **Pierre Renoir**'s, *The Promenade*, **Paul Cézanne**'s *The Card Players*, **Henri Rousseau**'s, *Woman Walking in Exotic Forest*, and **Georges Seurat**'s *Entrance to the Port of Honfleur*, all highly admired masterpieces of renown.

photo credit Shayne Ross

**THE BARNES COLLECTION**
*Philadelphia, PA USA*

**WOMAN WALKING IN AN EXOTIC FOREST**
*by Rousseau, Henri*

**LEDA AND THE SWAN**
*by Cezanne, Paul*

**MODELS**

*by Seurat, Georges*

**THE CARD PLAYERS (2)**

*by Cezanne, Paul*

**THE PROMENADE**
*by Renoir, Pierre Auguste*

**BEACH SCENE, GUERNSE**
*by Renoir, Pierre Auguste*

**ENTRANCE TO THE PORT OF HONFLEUR**

*by Seurat, Georges*

**HAERE PAPE**

*by Gauguin, Paul*

# The J. Paul Getty Museum

THE J. PAUL GETTY MUSEUM IS ACTUALLY TWO DISTINCTIVE SITES. ENJOYING A SEA BREEZE ON A HILLTOP IN MALIBU (WITH A PACIFIC PALISADES ADDRESS), THE GETTY VILLA IS ON PAR WITH ANY GREAT ROMAN VILLA. THE BUILDING AND GROUNDS ARE SPECTACULAR—WITH LUSH SCULPTURE GARDENS, TURQUOISE POOLS, AND SPARKLING FOUNTAINS, THE IDEAL SETTING FOR A COLLECTION DEDICATED TO ANTIQUITIES FROM ANCIENT GREECE, ROME, AND ETRURIA. THIS LOCATION ALSO SERVES AS A STATE-OF-THE-ART EDUCATIONAL CENTER.

The Getty Center, in Brentwood, contains a collection of Western art from the Middle Ages to the present, including some amazing European paintings. In addition to the famous *Irises* by **Vincent van Gogh**, other must-sees include **Titan**'s *Venus and Adonis*, **Edouard Manet**'s *Portrait of Madame Brunet*, and **Pierre Auguste Renoir**'s *La Promenade*. Some of *Prestige Fine Art*'s most beloved reproductions derive from paintings housed at the Getty.

photographer, Gunnar Kullenberg Rex/USA

**THE J. PAUL GETTY MUSEUM**
*Malibu, CA USA*

**YOUNG GIRL DEFENDING HERSELF AGAINST EROS**

*by Bouguereau, Adolphe William*

**IRISES**

*by Gogh, Vincent van*

**TWO WATERMILLS WITH AN OPEN SOURCE**
*by Ruisdael, Jacob van*

**COSIMO I DE'MEDICI**
*by Pontormo, Jacopo Carucci*

**DUTCH STILL LIFE: FLOWERS AND FRUIT**

*by Huysum, Jan van*

**VASE OF FLOWERS**

*by Huysum, Jan van*

**BASKET OF FLOWERS, 1614**
*by Bosschaert, Ambrosius (The Elder)*

**SPRING**
*by Alma-Tadema, Sir Lawrence*

**PORTRAIT OF MARIA FREDKE VAN REEDE-ATHLONE AT SEVEN YEARS**
*by Liotard, Jean-Etienne*

# Uffizi & Pitti Gallery

Birthplace of the Italian Renaissance, the fertile hotbed of artistic genius known as Florence is itself a museum. Still, the storied city boasts many actual museums--but none contain holdings of such exquisite beauty as the linked Uffizi and Pitti Galleries, rivaling any in the world.

Viewers at the Uffizi often start with **Giotto** and work their way to **Sandro Botticelli**; his *Birth of Venus* and *Primavera* are breathtaking. **Leonardo da Vinci**'s unfinished *Adoration of the Magi*, **Michelangelo's** *Doni Tondo*, and **Raphael** and **Caravaggio**'s masterworks deserve an afternoon, at least.

Home of the banking Pitti family and, during the 16th century, the ruling Medici family, Pitti Palace, designed by Duomo architect **Filippo Brunelleschi**, abounds with **Medici** acquisitions. Highlights include **Raphael**'s *La Donna Velata*, **Giorgione**'s *The Three Ages of Man*, and **Titan**'s *The Concert*. We at *Prestige Fine Art* have had the honor of recreating the following Uffizi and Pitti paintings.

photographer, Scott E. Barbour (The Image Bank) Getty Images

**The Uffizi & Pitti Gallery**
*Florence, Italy*

**BIRTH OF VENUS**

*by Botticelli, Alessandro di Mariano Filipepi*

**VIRGIN WITH A ROSARY**

*by Murillo, Bartolome*

**BACCHUS**

*by Caravaggio*

**DUCAL PALACE, VENICE**

*Canaletto, Giovanni Antonio*

**PORTRAIT OF ISABELLE DE'MEDICI**
*by Bronzino, Agnolo*

**SELF-PORTRAIT AS A YOUNG MAN**
*by Rembrandt, Harnensz, Van Rijn*

**PORTRAIT OF ANGELO DONI**

*by Raphael*

**LA DONNA VELATA**

*by Raphael*

# *Prestige Fine Art* Categories

We at *Prestige Fine Art* define our style categories in a unique and unexpected manner. We do not use the typical "art movement" terms that art historians or academics use. Instead, we have developed five category descriptions tailored to assist our art collectors. These are easily grasped terms that work, designed to break down the different artistic styles that we offer into straightforward language. Like so many things that look easy, it took us years to perfect these categories.

We always listen and learn from our customers. As a result, we have created categories that are of the most interest to our collectors, providing an uncomplicated point of reference to help them decide what types of paintings they like the most. Of course, we have plenty of cross-over genres, which fit into more than one category. Plus, we have devised subcategories to help define the most popular subject matter.

### Main Categories

Impressionism, Old Master Old World, Romantic Classical Victorian, Historical Western, Americana.

### These subcategories include:

Children, Nautical, Seascapes, Still Life, Hunting Scenes, Religious, Equestrian, Animals, Wildlife, Landscapes, Nudes, Floral, Street Scenes, Lovers, Pastels, Portraits, and more.

Remember, each of these subcategories can be applied to each of the five *Prestige Fine Art* style categories, which follow.

# Impressionism

*Prestige Fine Art*'s art category, "Impressionism", is the only term we use that is closely aligned with the term used in the academic and art historical worlds. It represents paintings created by the avant-garde artists of the 19<sup>th</sup> century; a time of groundbreaking changes in how artists saw the world around them. When collectors ask me, "What exactly does impressionism mean," I explain that the artists used a lot of color and vibrant strokes of paint applied quickly and thickly, thus creating a loose "impression" of a subject or scene rather than a detailed and highly refined study: think Monet, van Gogh, and Renoir.

**THE PINK DANCERS**

*by Degas, Edgar*

**THE DINNER PARTY (EMULATION)**

*by Grun, Jules Alexandre*

**THE PASSAGEWAY OF THE OPERA**

*by Beraud, Jean*

**PARIS STREET SCENE (EMULATION)**

*by Beraud, Jean*

**THE TWO SISTERS**

*by Renoir, Pierre Auguste*

**ARGENTEUIL**

*by Monet, Claude*

**SPRING BOUQUET**

*by Renoir, Pierre Auguste*

**DANS LA PRAIRIE**

*by Monet, Claude*

**SAILING BOAT AT ARGENTEUIL**

*by Caillebotte, Gustave*

**CHEZ LE PERE LATHUILE**

*by Manet, Edouard*

**OUTSIDE THE THEATER DU VAUDEVILLE (EMULATION)**

*by Beraud, Jean*

**MONET PAINTING IN HIS GARDEN IN ARGENTEUIL**

*by Renoir, Pierre Auguste*

**NATURE MORTE:LES GROSSES POMMES**

*by Cezanne, Paul*

**THE GARDENS OF LES MATHURINS AT PONTOISE, 1876**

*by Pissarro, Camille*

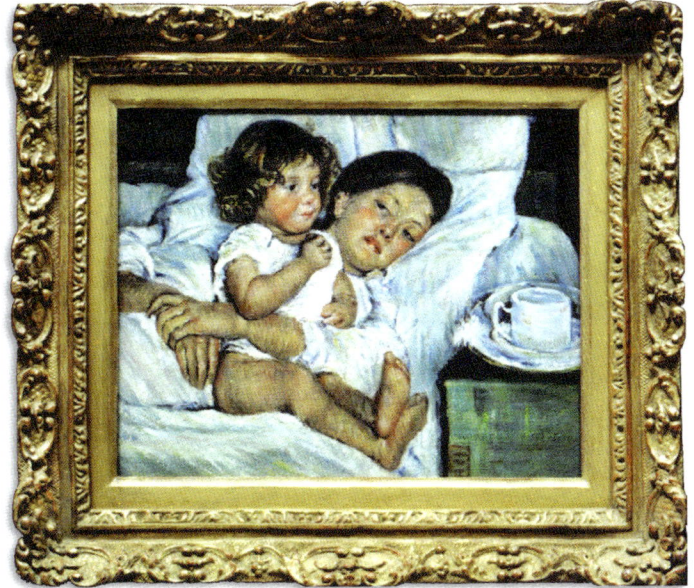

**BREAKFAST IN BED**

*by Cassatt, Mary*

**CALM MORNING**

*by Benson, Frank Weston*

**SIDEWALK CAFE AT NIGHT**
*by Gogh, Vincent van*

**SEASCAPE AT SAINTE-MARIES
(VIEW OF MEDITERRANEAN)**
*by Gogh, Vincent van*

**THE DUCK POND**
*by Monet, Claude*

**THE APPLE SELLER**
*by Renoir, Pierre Auguste*

# Old Master Old World

OLD MASTER/OLD WORLD, IN *PRESTIGE FINE ART* TERMINOLOGY, IS BEST DESCRIBED AS THE ARTISTIC STYLES AND ARTISTS OF THE 16TH CENTURY, SUCH AS REMBRANDT, DA VINCI, CARAVAGGIO (AND MANY MORE). THESE PAINTINGS TEND TO BE DARK IN COLOR AND FILLED WITH PAINTERLY TEXTURE. WE ARE HIGHLY SKILLED AT RECREATING THESE ASPECTS, AND WE CAN ALSO "AGE" SUCH PAINTINGS TO MAKE THEM LOOK EVEN OLDER AND MORE AUTHENTIC. PRIMARILY, OUR COLLECTORS UNDERSTAND THAT THIS CATEGORY REFERS TO THE RENOWNED "OLD MASTERS" OF THE PREDOMINANTLY EUROPEAN "OLD WORLD".

**ADORATION OF THE MAGI**

*by Rubens, Peter Paul*

**WOMAN WITH A PEARL NECKLACE**

*by Vermeer, Jan*

**SHEPHERDS WITH HER FLOCK**

*by Millet, Jean-Francois*

**THE STORM ON THE SEA OF GALILEE**

*by Rembrandt Harmensz, van Rijn*

**ST. MICHAEL**

*by Murillo, Bartolome*

**SEAPORT WITH THE EMBARKATION OF THE QUEEN OF SABA**

*by Lorraine, Claude*

**GRAND CANAL THE RIALTO BRIDGE FROM THE NORTH**

*by Canaletto (Giovanni Antonio Canal)*

**THE ASTRONOMER**

*by Vermeer, Jan*

**THE ANGELUS**

*by Millet, Jean-Francois*

**THE CROWNING OF SAINT CATHERINE**

*by Rubens, Peter Paul*

**THE RETURN OF THE PRODIGAL SON**

*by Rembrandt Harmensz, van Rijn*

**FRUIT AND BIRDS**

*by Bogdany, Jakob*

133

**GALLERY WITH A VIEW OF ANCIENT ROME**
*by Pannini, Giovanni Paolo*

**THE GARDEN OF LOVE**
*by Rubens, Peter Paul*

**THE TRIUMPH OF ALEXANDER**

*by Lebrun, Charles*

**THE TRIBUNA OF THE UFFIZI**

*by Zoffany, John*

**THE ALLEGORY OF PAINTING**

*by Vermeer, Jan*

**BUCINTORO RETURNING TO THE MOLO ON ACENSION**

*by Canaletto (Giovanni Antonio Canal)*

# Romantic Classical Victorian

THIS CATEGORY ENCOMPASSES MANY GENRES THAT CROSS OVER AMONG THE MAIN *PRESTIGE FINE ART* CATEGORIES. "ROMANTIC" INCLUDES WORKS BY MANY DIFFERENT ARTISTS WHO ALL FOCUS ON SUBJECTS IMBUED WITH A LOVING NATURE. "CLASSICAL" REFERS TO ANY PAINTINGS THAT CONJURE AN ETERNAL GRAVITAS, ESPECIALLY A SIGNIFICANT TIME PERIOD OR EVENT IN HISTORY--OFTEN PAINTED BY MASTERS WHO SPECIALIZE IN THE GENRE. "VICTORIAN" CAPTURES AN ERA WHEN ARTISTS PAINTED WOMEN AND LANDSCAPES HIGHLIGHTED BY DECORATIVE FRILLS AND FLOURISHES, WHETHER IN MANNER OF DRESS OR EXPRESSION OF SCENERY.

**THE MERMAID**

*by Leighton, Frederic--Lord of Stretton*

**THE SWING**

*by Fragonard, Jean-Honore*

**BANQUET STILL LIFE WITH PARROTS**

*by de Heem, Jan Davidz*

**CIRCE**

*by Wardle, Arthur*

**PREPARATIONS FOR THE MARRIAGE
OF THE SHERIF'S DAUGHTERS**

*by Tapiro y Bara, Jose*

**THE LION HUNT**

*by Delacroix, Eugene*

**THE STOLEN KISS**

*by Fragonard, Jean-Honore*

**THE MUSICAL CONTEST**

*by Fragonard, Jean-Honore*

**THE GUITAR PLAYER**

*by Vermeer, Jan*

**VERMEER IN HIS STUDIO**

*by Charlemont, Eduard*

**ROMEO & JULIET**

*by Dicksee, Sir Frank*

**LADY GODIVA**

*by Collier, John (The Honorable)*

**REST, 1879**

*by Bouguereau, Adolphe William*

**ABDUCTION OF PSYCHE**

*by Bouguereau, Adolphe William*

**UNCONSCIOUS RIVALS**

*by Alma-Tadema, Sir Lawrence*

**THE RECITAL**

*by Riggiani*

**A Sculpture Gallery**
*by Alma-Tadema, Sir Lawrence*

**Song of the Angels, 1881**
*by Bouguereau, Adolphe William*

**AURORA**

*by Reni, Guido*

**MARS DISARMED BY VENUS AND THE THREE GRACES**

*by David, Jacques-Louis*

# Historical and Western

"HISTORICAL", TO THE FOLKS AT *PRESTIGE FINE ART*, MEANS PAINTINGS THAT SIGNIFY EVENTS IN THE WORLD THAT MERIT RECOGNITION AND HAVE BEEN DOCUMENTED BY A WELL-KNOWN ARTIST. IT IS A BROAD CATEGORY THAT ENCOMPASSES ITS OWN DISTINCTIVE SET OF SUBCATEGORIES: RELIGIOUS, WAR, INDEPENDENCE, CULTURAL EVENTS, AND SOCIETAL CHANGES. THESE PAINTINGS REPRESENT MONUMENTAL MOMENTS CAPTURED BY MONUMENTAL ARTISTS.

The category, "Western", indicates the American West, a grand and panoramic style of painting that celebrates pioneers, cowboys, Native Americans, and the sweeping and spectacular natural vistas that make up our vast country. This category is ideal for art lovers who are intrigued by six shooters, spurs, and cowboy hats--and riding the prairies and plains of the old West on galloping horses--evoking a way of life that was both challenging and romantic.

**WASHINGTON READING HIS FAREWELL ADDRESS**
*by Moran Edward Percy*

**THE LAST SUPPER**
*by da Vinci, Leonardo*

**A Dash for the Timbers**

*by Remington Frederic*

**Defeat of the Spanish Armada**

*by Vroom, Hendrick Cornelisz*

**THE BATTLE OF WATERLOO, 1815**

*Prestige Fine Art*

**CAVALRY CHARGES ON THE SOUTHERN PLAINS**

*by Remington, Frederic*

**NAPOLEON ADDRESSING THE SECOND CORP OF THE GRAND ARMY**

*by Gautherot, Pierre*

**NEPTUNE RESIGNING TO BRITANNIA THE EMPIRE OF THE SEA**

*by Dyce, William*

**WHEN THE LAW DULLS THE EDGE OF CHANCE**

*by Russell, Charles M.*

**THE SERMON ON THE MOUNT**

*by Bloch, Carl Heinrich*

**LOOPS AND SWIFT HORSES ARE SURER THAN LEAD**
*by Russell, Charles M*

**ATTACK ON THE SUPPLY WAGONS**
*by Remington, Frederic*

**THE CINCH RING**
*by Russell, Charles M.*

**IN WITHOUT KNOCKING**
*by Russell, Charles M*

**THE AMBUSH**
*by Russell, Charles M.*

**THE TROOPER**
*by Remington, Frederic*

**BOMBARDMENT OF ALGIERS**
*by Chambers, George*

**THE CAPTURE CONSTANTINOPLE**
*by Tintoretto, Jocopo Robusti*

**JUSTICE**
*by Anonymous*

**BONAPARTE CROSSING THE ALPS**
*by David, Jacques-Louis*

# Americana

THIS CATEGORY DOCUMENTS AMERICAN HISTORY, FROM EARLY AMERICAN HISTORY, SUCH AS THE LANDING OF CHRISTOPHER COLUMBUS, TO THE PRESENT DAY, SUCH AS THE LANDING ON THE MOON. IN SHORT, IT REFERENCES THE STRUGGLES AND TRIUMPHS THAT AMERICA HAS EXPERIENCED IN ITS MORE THAN 200 YEARS OF EXISTENCE. THESE PAINTINGS SHOUT, "THIS IS THE AMERICAN WAY OF LIFE!"

**OLD MODELS**

*by Harnett, William Michael*

**THE OLD VIOLIN**

*by Harnett, William Michael*

**THE YACHT MAGIC DEFENDAING AMERICA'S CUP, 1870**

*by Buttersworth, James Edward*

**TAKING HIS EASE, 1885**

*by Hovenden, Thomas*

**PRIDE**

*by Hovenden, Thomas*

**TENDING THE ROSE GARDEN**
*by Knight, Daniel Ridgway*

**SNAP THE WHIP**
*by Homer, Winslow*

**SOUTH BOSTON PIER**
*by Prendergast, Maurice*

**THREE BOYS IN LOBSTER BOAT**
*by Homer, Winslow*

**SIERRA NEVADA**
*by Bierstadt, Albert*

**A ROCKY TORRENT - GRAND CANYON**
*by Moran, Thomas*

**WATERFALL**

*by Smith, John Brandon*

**MRS. FISKE WARREN AND HER DAUGHTER RACHEL**

*by Sargent, John Singer*

**INDEPENDENCE (SQUIRE JACK PORTER)**

*by Mayer, Frank Blackwell*

**STUDY OF AN ORCHID**

*by Heade, Martin Johnson*

**KINDRED SPIRITS**

*by Durand, Asher Brown*

**GRAND CANYON WITH RAINBOW**

*by Moran, Thomas*

**BAHAMAS HARBOUR, 1882**
*by Bierstadt, Albert*

**THE CONSUMMATION OF EMPIRE (COURSE OF THE EMPIRE SERIES)**
*by Cole, Thomas*

**THE AVENUE IN THE RAIN**

*by Hassam, Frederick Childe*

**STATUE OF LIBERTY ENLIGHTENING THE WORLD**

*by Moran, Edward*

# Pastels

----------

IT HAS ALWAYS BEEN MY DESIRE TO SHARE AND ENJOY ALL THE POPULAR MEDIUMS OF ART. "PASTELS" HAVE BEEN USED BY MANY RENOWNED ARTISTS, FROM DEGAS TO PICASSO, AND THEY ARE A JOYFUL, LIGHTHEARTED, AND ENLIGHTENING EXAMPLE OF ART WORKS THAT STEP OUTSIDE THE REALM OF THE OIL PAINTING MEDIUM.

Over the years, we have engaged our talented artists to recreate famous pastels, drawings, and even photographs to enhance our loyal art patrons' individual collections. Here is a small sampling of some of the fine works in pastel that *Prestige Fine Art* has produced, honoring the medium's brilliant color palette and unrestrained expressiveness.

**ORCHARD SURROUNDED BY CYPRESSES**

*by Gogh, Vincent van*

**THE SOWER**

*by Gogh, Vincent van*

**DANCERS AT THE BARRA, 1877-79**

*by Degas, Edgar*

**LES BALLERINES**

*by Degas, Edgar*

**YOUNG WOMAN WIAA DANCER WITH TAMBOURINE**

*by Degas, Edgar*

**DANSEUSE**

*by Degas, Edgar*

# Portraits

---

*Prestige Fine Art* Painting Categories

*"To give body and perfect form to your thought, this alone is what it is to be an artist."*
*--Jacques-Louis David*

Artists have been painting portraits for centuries.  This genre captures a moment in time, visually documenting for posterity the individuals who have shaped our world.  Portrait galleries in every country are filled with portraits of emperors, presidents, noblemen, inventors, scientists, religious figures, financial barons, as well as kings and queens.  The artists who painted them, and the people who commissioned them, wished to create a legacy of how they made their mark on history.

It is no surprise that one of the staples of many an artist's body of work has often been portraiture.  These artists took the path of painting portraits of prominent or royal figures as a means of supporting themselves well while bringing joy to their sitters.  Likewise, wealthy individuals have long sought out celebrated portrait artists, known for their talent at capturing the spirit of their subjects through facial expressions and bodily gestures--giving the viewer a glimpse of the "real" person behind the crown, title, or family name.

Artists also paint self-portraits as a way of securing their own legacy. Several artists, such as **Rembrandt**, 1606-1669, painted numerous self-portraits at different stages of their lives. I will never forget sitting on a viewing bench in the Metropolitan Museum of Art during an exhibition of many such paintings by the Dutch painter. As I sat contemplating this great artist, I felt as though he was staring straight at me from everywhere I looked.

SELF-PORTRAIT AT THE AGE OF **34**
*by Rembrandt Harmensz, van Rijn*

The eyes in **Rembrandt**'s self-portraits are particularly haunting and memorable. While you are observing his eyes, you get the distinct feeling that he is looking at you! He seems to be challenging you with his extraordinary talent, and the viewer gets a glimpse of this special artist's true personality. We can see clearly why Rembrandt's depth and perception set the bar for the artists of his time.

German portrait painter **Franz Winterhalter** was very prolific and well known for his likenesses of royalty painted in the mid-nineteenth century, and his name became associated with fashionable court portraiture. Among his best known works are *Empress Eugénie Surrounded by her Ladies in Waiting* (1855) and *Empress Elisabeth of Austria* (1865); one of several portraits of this monarch.

**Winterhalter** painted hundreds of portraits for his Victoria-era patrons. Some were portraits of illustrious individuals or families; others were portraits of titled ladies and gentlemen or monarchs of the day. Before cameras came along, portraits served the purpose of recording images to honor and preserve the memories of the movers

ROYAL FAMILY
*by Winterhalter Franz*

and shakers of a particular time. Philosophers, teachers, writers, scientists, poets, captains, generals, admirals--all of these renowned men and women grace the walls of national portrait galleries throughout the world—a visual "who's who" chronicling the important faces and figures that comprise history.

During the march for freedom of colonial America, we were graced with portrait artists such as **John Trumbull**, **Rembrandt Peale**, and many more. Even with the availability of modern-day photography, painted portraits remain a very popular medium. There is something painterly and evocative about a hand-painted portrait that a photograph is unable to replicate. The depth of a hand-painted portrait by a skilled artist is truly a marvel that inspires admiration.

Like other forms of painting, such as landscapes and still-life paintings, portraits are painted in many different styles. These include impressionism, photo realism, abstraction, cubism, and much more. Many artists, such as **John Singer Sargent, John Trumbull, Charles Wilson Peale**, and the aforementioned **Franz Winterhalter**, developed signature portrait styles over time, which are immediately recognizable. These specialty artists were sought out by "suitors" who wanted a portrait painted by a well-known portrait master. They also painted subjects of their own liking, which further displayed their talents, but they were often called upon to paint portraits for which they had garnered top-notch reputations.

In my career as an art dealer, I have enjoyed learning about these great masters of portraits. I have visited numerous museums and galleries whose collections are dedicated to portraiture.

Portraits painted by the living masters of today can command prices in the tens-of- thousands to hundreds-of-thousands of dollars. I have known modern portrait masters who require a minimum of fifty thousand dollars, and they have a three-year waiting list.

Our artists at *Prestige Fine Art* offer portraits at very reasonable rates without compromising expertise and excellence. We have had clients request copies of celebrated presidential portraits, famous family portraits, and well-known royal portraits, along with their own

CONWAY WEDDING PORTRAIT
*by Prestige Fine Art*

portraits or portraits of their children and grandchildren. These personal portraits become exceptional keepsakes of heirloom quality that mark a client's, or his or her family's, own "moment in time."

What's more, our artists can easily work from photographs if a subject cannot sit for a portrait. In this way, our artists can also capture entire families experiencing momentous occasions. For instance, one such family had visited Machu Picchu in Peru and wanted the magical journey captured for all time. Another client commissioned a wedding portrait as a gift from father-to-bride. These are milestone moments in the lives of families, depicted in a unique way and passed down from generation to generation.

PORTRAIT OF MARK & JOANN SKOUSEN WITH SON AT MACHU PICCHU
*by Prestige Fine Art*

Our artists' ability to work from photographs not only gives our clients the flexibility of not having to sit for hours on end, but also allows the artist to romanticize and idealize the painting (if that is what a client desires). For example, an artist might paint an engagement ring diamond a few carats larger than the real thing or help the groom shed a few pounds for his wedding day! Again, this would be done only upon request. The following pages of *Prestige Fine Art's* distinctive portrait work will give you an idea of how you might create your own portrait of a loved one or of an historical figure you personally admire. In short, portraits stand the test of time and offer years of enjoyment throughout the generations.

Here's a notable story. A client requested life-sized portraits of the first four presidents of the United States for the Founders Inn in Virginia Beach. We also painted 100 works of art for this historic hotel's learning center. This was our client's response to the portraits:

*"The standing portrait of Washington is nothing short of magnificent! I doubt if even an expert could tell that it is not an original."* --Pat Robertson, Chairman of the Board

We have had requests from individuals to paint portraits of beloved inventors and scientists, too. For example, our artists painted portraits of the father of modern chemistry, Antoine-Laurent de Lavoisier, American inventor Thomas Edison, French chemist and biologist Louis Pasteur (responsible for the pasteurization process), and French-Polish physicist, chemist, and Nobel Prize winner Marie Currie, famous for her pioneering research on radioactivity. These portraits were intended for an art collection dedicated to the great inventors and scientists behind the world's most life-changing breakthroughs.

**PORTRAIT OF THOMAS EDISON**
*by Prestige Fine Art*

**PORTRAIT OF MARIE CURIE**
*by Prestige Fine Art*

**PORTRAIT OF LOUIS PASTEUR**
*by Prestige Fine Art*

**PORTRAIT OF LAVOISIER**
*by Prestige Fine Art*

Portraiture is a difficult art form, requiring special skills developed over many years of study, and *Prestige Fine Art* has many brilliant portrait artists at its disposal to fulfill the need for such a specialized art form. Within this realm, as we do within other painting categories, we offer many customized painting options for our art lovers and collectors. Our ability to deliver distinctive and exceptional portraits is another example of how *Prestige Fine Art* enhances lives by providing meaning through the power of art.

**PORTRAIT OF JAMES MADISON**
*by Vanderlyn, John*

**JOHN ADAMS**
*by Peale, Charles Willson*

**ABRAHAM LINCOLN**
*by Story, G. H*

**THOMAS JEFFERSON**
*by Peale, Rembrandt*

**GEORGE WASHINGTON**
*by Peale, Rembrandt*

**PORTRAIT OF SAM HOUSTON**
*by Prestige Fine Art*

**PORTRAIT OF BENJAMIN FRANKLIN**
*by Greuze, Jean Baptise*

**SELF PORTRAIT JOHN TRUMBULL**
*by Trumbull, John*

**PRINCE ALBERT**
*by Winterhalter Franz*

**PORTRAIT OF WOLFGANG AMADEUS MOZART**
*by Krafft, Barbara*

**THE MEETING OF JACOB AND RACHEL**
*by Dyce, William*

**BROTHER & SISTER**
*by Beechey, Sir William*

**JESUS CHRIST**
*by Prestige Fine Art*

**ART & LITERATURE, 1867**
*by Bouguereau, Adolphe William*

**PHILADELPHIA AND ELIZABETH WHARTON**
*by Dyck, Sir Anthony Van*

**QUEEN VICTOARIA
AT HER CORONATION, 1838**
*by Hayter, George*

**LA PEINTURE EN PLEIN AIR**
*by Vanaise, Gustave*

**DAISIES**
*by Bouguereau, Adolphe William*

**THE ASCENSION OF CHRIST**

*by Rembrandt Harmensz, van Rijn*

**A BOY READING (TITUS)**

*by Rembrandt Harmensz, van Rijn*

**ARISTOTLE CONTEMPLATING THE BUST OF HOMER**

*by Rembrandt Harmensz, van Rijn*

**SELF-PORTRAIT AS A YOUNG MAN**

*by Rembrandt Harmensz, van Rijn*

**HENRY HOWARD, EARL OF SURREY**

*by Scrotes, Guillim*

**PORTRAIT OF A YOUNG MAN**

*by Bonvicino, Alessandro*

**PORTRAIT OF A MAN**

*by Messina, Antonello da*

**PORTRAIT OF A YOUNG MAN**

*by Bellini, Giovanni*

**HER NEW LOVE**

*by Elsley, Arthur John*

**A GIRL WITH A BASKET OF FRUIT**

*by Leighton, Frederic-Lord of Stretton*

**THE BLUE BOY**

*by Gainsborough, Thomas*

**PINKIE**

*by Lawrence, Sir Thomas*

**SIR ARTHUR CONAN DOYLE**

*by Gates, H. L*

**THE FIRST OF MAY, 1851**

*by Winterhalter, Xavier*

**EMPRESS JOSEPHINE OF FRANCE #2**

*by Gerard, Francois*

**PORTRAIT OF A WOMAN WITH BLACK TIE**

*by Modigliani, Amedeo*

**PORTRAIT OF A KNIGHT OF MALTA**

*by Caravaggio*

**DAISIES**

*by Bouguereau, Adolphe William*

**CONWAY WEDDING PORTRAIT**
*by Prestige Fine Art*

**PORTRAIT OF DONALD TRUMP**
*by Prestige Fine Art*

**PORTRAIT OF THE LATHAM'S**
*by Prestige Fine Art*

**PORTRAIT OF MR. &
MRS. DeROSA**
*by Prestige Fine Art*

**PORTRAIT OF TRACY & BRITTANY**
*by Prestige Fine Art*

**PORTRAIT OF ELLY**
*by Prestige Fine Art*

**PORTRAIT OF JAMES KENNY**
*by Prestige Fine Art*

**PORTRAIT OF
MRS. VAN SPALL**
*by Prestige Fine Art*

**PORTRAIT OF JACQUIE MERO**
*by Prestige Fine Art*

**PORTRAIT OF THE
ETZEL CHILDREN**
*by Prestige Fine Art*

**PORTRAIT OF MRS. OSHEROW**
*by Prestige Fine Art*

**PORTRAIT OF NICOLE AND
JACQUIE MERO**
*by Prestige Fine Art*

**PORTRAIT OF TYLER PERRY**
*by Ron DiScenza*

**PORTRAIT OF ELMER AND
NATALIE MERO**
*by Prestige Fine Art*

# Sculpture

_"I saw the Angel in the marble and carved until I set him free."_

_Michelangelo_

SCULPTURE THROUGH THE CENTURIES HAS BEEN ADMIRED BY ART LOVERS AND ENHANCES MUSEUM COLLECTIONS AROUND THE WORLD. I HAVE EXPERIENCED SHEER JOY IN VIEWING AND OWNING MANY DIFFERENT WORLD-CLASS SCULPTURES THAT ARE ACTUALLY COPIES OF HIGHLY REGARDED ARTISTS, SUCH AS **BERNINI**, **RODIN**, **DEGAS**, **CANOVA**, **MICHELANGELO**, **BOTTICELLI**, TO NAME ONLY A FEW. OVER THE YEARS, WE AT _PRESTIGE FINE ART_ HAVE SOUGHT OUT COMPANIES AND INDIVIDUAL ARTISTS WHO CAN DELIVER WHAT OUR COLLECTORS LONG TO POSSESS.

**A FRIDAY AT THE SALON OF THE FRENCH ARTISTS**
_by Grun, Jules Alexandre_

## The Eleganza Collection

For many years we worked with The Eleganza Collection, which specializes in museum-quality reproductions of sculptural masterpieces. This fine company supplied many of our needs for more than a decade.

**BALLERINA II**
by Canova, Antonio
(1757-1822)

**LOVE AND PSYCHE**
by Canova, Antonio
(1757 - 1822)

**PYGMALION AND GALATEA**
by Gerome, Jean-Leon
**Painting (sculpture creation)**

**MERCURY**
by Bologna, da Giovanni
(1524 - 1609)

**THE KISS**
by Rodin, Auguste
(1840 - 1917)

# Eric Stepeniewski

**Eric Stepeniewski** is an artist associate whom I have worked with for many years, and it has been a privilege. He is a master craftsman well-known for creating fine candelabras, tables, vases, chandeliers, sconces, and other decorative objects. Accented with stones such as malachite, lapis lazuli, and various marbles, these objects of art are fit for a museum. Many of his pieces are blends of brass and 24-karat gilded gold, as well as crystal, glass, and stone. **Eric** is able to produce anything you wish from an original piece, or from a photograph or a good drawing. His repertoire contains true works of art made with a degree of style and detail that rivals items in The Barron Collection.

www.ericstepniewski.pl

These are several of Eric's Creations
Candelabras, Tables, Vases, Chandeliers, Sconces , and other decorative objects.

The newest addition to our sculpture offerings derives from Masterpiece Investments, which carries many different sculptures. Masterpiece Investments is a partner of AIDA Founderia Historica Chiurazzi, a sculpture foundry that was established in the 1800s and entrusted to make plaster molds from original marble sculptures found in world-class museums—including the Uffizi, Villa Borghese, the Louvre, the Vatican collection, and many others.

Today Chiurazzi possesses more than 1,500 original master molds from the most famous museums in the world, and the most famous artists in history, including **Michelangelo, Bernini, Deletano, Canova, Giambologna**, and **Cellini**. This organization is truly a magnificent affiliate for *Prestige Fine Art*, enabling us to better enrich the sculpture collections of our devoted clientele.

**Victory of Samothrace**

One of the most superb works of Hellenistic art, between the IV or beginning of the III century B.C. This renowned masterpiece of unknown authorship was collocated on the prow of the ship of Demetrius Poliorcetes, after gaining his great naval victory over the fleet of Ptolemy Soter at Salamis.

*(Limited Edition Bronze and Pure Silver Originals)*
200 cm

**Venus de Milo**

An outstanding sculpture from the III century B.C. by an unknown artist, probably by Agessandro or Alexander of Antiocha. In this celebrated statue of the Aphrodite the artist has shown in all its splendor the ideal woman form as goddess of Beauty and Love.

*(Limited Edition Bronze and Pure Silver Originals)*
204 cm

**Perseus**

Celebrated group of the famous goldsmith Benvenuto Cellini. The hero has perfectly executed the order to kill Medusa. He proudly shows the severed head and stamps on the body. The base is richly decorated and displays four gods: Giove, Minerva, Mercury, and Danae.

*(Limited Edition Bronze and Pure Silver Originals)*
200 cm

**Rape of Proserpina**

One of the most admired works of Bernini. Pluto is in the act of carrying off the daughter of Demeter. The Rape of Proserpina depicts the abduction of the young daughter of Ceres by Pluto. Pluto falls in love with Proserpina, abducts her, and takes her to his home in the underworld.

*(Limited Edition Bronze and Pure Silver Originals)*
255 cm

**Laocoon**

One of the most discussed and famous group of Hellinistic art, defined by Michaelangelo as a prodigy of art. This original work of Rhodian artist Agessandro, II century B.C. depicts Laocoon, a Troyan priest of Apollo, who dared to dissuade against drawing the wooden horse into the city of Troy. He was, together with his two sons, condemned by the anger of the gods to be crushed to death by serpents.

*(Limited Edition Bronze and Pure Silver Originals)*
*(Michaelangelo's finished version)*
240 cm

## Masterpiece Investments – Lorenzo Ghiglieri

Another talent who contributes to our sculpture catalog is **Lorenzo Ghiglieri** of Masterpiece Investments. His original creations grace the most prestigious museums and art collections in the world. The White House, Vatican, Kremlin, and the Royal Palace in Madrid are just a few venues for his works.

*"The eye and the hand of the Master"*

*Lorenzo E. Ghiglieri*

World renowned artist and sculptor, Lorenzo Ghiglieri, has creations gracing the most prestigious museums and art collections around the world. The

Pieta
by Michelangelo
St Peters Basilica in Vatican, Rome

## Nilda Maria Comas

LIFE B, 2000 MARBLE HEIGHT 25"
*by Nilda Maria Comas*

*Agopoff Prize, National Sculpture Society,2000 Charlotte Dunwiddie Memorial Award for Tradional sculpture 2004.*

As previously mentioned, we honor the original works of artists as well as their recreated works. Another sculptor whom we work with is **Nilda Maria Comas**. **Nilda** was born in San Juan, Puerto Rico, and she earned her fine arts degree at the University of Houston. While traveling, she discovered Pietrasanta, an artist colony in Italy, and she spent time there learning the techniques of bronze casting. **Nilda** worked alongside artists such as **Lucchesi** and **Joseph Sheppard** who encouraged her to attend the New York Academy of Figurative Art.

She received the highest scholarship given by the Academy and went on to graduate cum laude with a Masters in Fine Art. She has said, "My preferential interest, as an artist, is the creation of figurative sculpture and

IN A MARBLE CAVE
*by Nilda Maria Comas*
Carra, Comas (center) and
Franco Cerviette (right)
*Italy*

PALM BEACH GIRL 1998 BRONZE
*by Nilda Maria Comas*
*height 32" Best in Show, Westminster Exhibition of Women artist, London,2003*

LI'L BLADDER
*by Nilda Comas*
*(donated by Howard Stillman Bates)*
*Colee Hammock Park, Ft Lauderdale*

painting resulting in a three-dimensional commentary on the human spirit. Fine art, which is well conceived and properly executed, leads us all to grow more compassionate, as the figure created communicates to the viewer a cleaner understanding of what it is to be human."

Today **Nilda** continues to divide her time between Pietrasanta and Fort Lauderdale, teaching and practicing her craft. Every year she takes a group of artists to Italy to immerse them in the experience of a lifetime. It was while taking her classes that I had a great inspiration. As a result, we are proud to offer special portrait commissions by **Nilda**, either painted or sculpted, as well as many of her original masterpieces.

In addition, **Nilda** has participated in a unique project that we also represent, which consists of eight or more sculptures (she has already created several) that will travel to several museums throughout the world. Titled ***Nilda Comas*** *Kiss Series*, each sculpture is enhanced

## The Kiss Collection

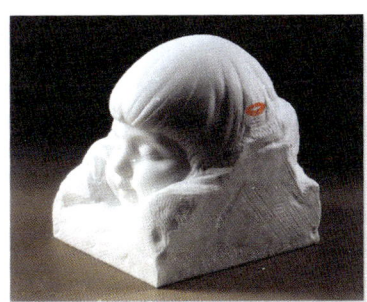

SLEEPING CHILD
*by Nilda Comas*

MELANCOLIA **2000** MARBLE
*by Nilda Maria Comas*
*height 19" Agopoff Prize, National Sculpture Society 2000*

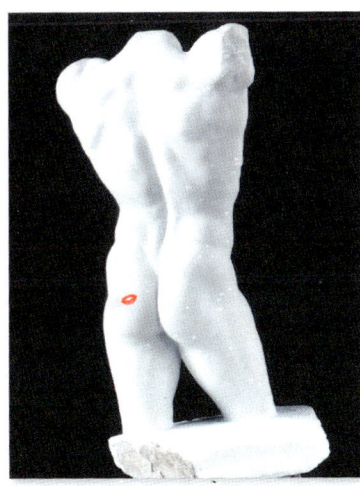

VICTORY, **1999**
*by Nilda Maria Comas*
marble 37 x 20 x 24 *From "The Kiss" series*

LAST MOMENTS
*by Nilda Comas*

with lips and is designed to touch the viewer's heart and imagination—and worthy of any of the major museums described in this book.

> *The true value of making art for me as an artist begins with self-revelation. Artwork serves many functions in Society. Perhaps, the most central is that of communication. The production of "The Kiss Collection" will communicate the many forms of kissing, one of the most beautiful acts of humanity, in a technique that is traditional, exploring the illicit and proper and the forbidden and condones aspects of kissing.*
>
> ### Nilda Comas

Sculpture is a highly skilled art form. It requires a sculptor's grand vision and a lifetime of dedication. With its ancient roots, sculpture continues to evolve in the current age and will surely make its mark beyond our lifetime, well into the distant future—utilizing materials that do not even exist yet! As we continue to admire the great artistic works of the past and present, sculpture has a well-deserved place in every art enthusiast's dream collection.

# Photography And Photorealism

Since its advent, photography has intrigued admirers of the arts. Photographs give us the ability to enter the mind of the photographer and see what he or she sees through the camera's lens. These images, captured moments in time, live on—clearly making fine photography an esteemed art form. Richard Polsky's new book, *The Art Prophets*, documents all of the great artists, art dealers, and taste makers who have rocked the art world, then and now, and great photographers are among them.

While an art form in its own right, photography also serves as a tool to help many painters better see and remember—and photographs influence painters and vice a versa. As one example: there is a genre of paintings known as photorealism, whose practitioners create canvases that look exactly like enlarged photographs, demonstrating an amazing aptitude for detail. Likewise, many photographers attempt to create photographs that look painterly.

Art dealer and "founder" of photorealism **Louis K. Meisel**, whose gallery is in Soho, New York, helped to establish an understanding of the photorealism movement with his comprehensive books on the subject, the first one published in 1980. In Meisel's view, as stated during an interview conducted by Polsky, "Photorealism affected the thinking of artists such as **Jeff Koons** and **Richard Prince**, who blew up photographs rather than paint them." These artists and others such as **Andy Warhol**, **Mel Ramos**, and **Chuck Close**, have all pioneered the use of incorporating photorealism in their work in various degrees.

Likewise, great photographers such as **Helmut Newton**, **Ansel Adams**, **Annie Liebovitz**, and **Alfred Eisenstaedt** (known for his famous 1945 photograph, *The Kissing Sailor*) have used their photography as artistic expression, sharing their vision and creativity through this art form alone. On a recent trip to Italy, I was impressed to find a large format book of **Helmut Newton**'s photographs placed in a prominent spot of the lobby of the hotel in which I was staying. Each page displayed photograph after photograph of his work inspired by a multitude of subjects, each image a thought-provoking, stand-alone photograph—all of them viewed together a profound vision. Whether photographing fashion, nudes, the beach, you name it, **Newton** was a master.

TASCHEN BOOK ON DISPLAY IN BOUTIQUE HOTEL
*Florence, Italy*

INSIDE COVER OF TASCHEN COLLECTOR BOOK SIGNED
*by Helmut Newton*

STAND AVAILABE TO DISPLAY ART & PHOTOGRAPHY BOOKS
*by Taschen*

The museums of the world feature photography in their permanent collections and in special photography exhibitions. As fine art and technology continue to evolve and merge, we are seeing more and more photography exhibition at museums. The auction houses of Sotheby's and Christie's also reflect this interest with a resurgence of demand for artistic photography.

On my most recent visit to San Diego, California, I was delighted to spend time with an underwater diver and photographer named **Michael Poirier** (born in 1946). He has been diving since he was 14 years old, and in 2002 he created a DVD presentation of his exploits deep in the waters of Indonesia, Hawaii, Bali, the Philippines, and Fiji. He had taken still shots of underwater coral reefs and exotic fish that are nothing short of some of the finest art work I have ever seen. The colors, detail, and motion that he captured with his underwater camera evoke emotion in the same way that great paintings do, and I used my visit to tell him so.

LIONFISH IN CORAL
*by Mike Poirier*

MIKE POIRIER
*Artist/Photographer underwater diver/ adventure*

CLOWN FISH
*by Mike Poirier*

LONGJAW SQUIRRELFISH WITH CORAL WALL
*by Mike Poirier*

CLOWN FISH IN CORAL
*by Mike Poirier*

With the use of Photoshop techniques, many photographers can now enhance their captured images to create artwork that is visually forward thinking and utterly stunning. In addition, many artists of the 21st century are utilizing this new technology in other ways, taking images that they have captured with their cameras and then going into the studio to create paintings, sculptures, or other multi-media art, inspired by the original images.

*Prestige Fine Art* believes that art collectors should embrace all forms of art and enjoy mixing various mediums to stimulate all of the senses. Photography in its pure form, or as a powerful component of other art forms, as well as photorealistic paintings, are all waiting to be explored by the venturesome art connoisseur--and added to his or her art collection.

# Collecting Original Art

*"Through a painting we can see the whole world."*

**--Hans Hofmann**

MUCH HAS BEEN SAID AND WRITTEN ABOUT COLLECTING ORIGINAL ART. THE PRICE OF ART, WHETHER SOLD IN THE PRIMARY OR THE SECONDARY MARKET, IS GOVERNED BY SUPPLY, DEMAND, AND MARKETING. A QUOTE ATTRIBUTED TO EMILY HALL TREMAINE (1908-1987), ONE OF AMERICA'S TOP COLLECTORS OF 20TH CENTURY ART, SUMS IT UP:

*"A collector has one of three motives for collecting: a genuine love of art, the investment possibilities, or its social promise. I have never known a collector who was not stimulated by all three. For the full joy and reward, the dominant motivation must be the love of art, but I would question the integrity of any collector who denies an interest in the valuation the market puts on his pictures. The social aspect is another never-ending regard. From Rome to Tokyo, our interest has brought unexpected and unbelievable experiences, and friends as full of vitality, imagination, and warmth as the art they collect."*

Fine art for the collector can, in some cases, be purchased directly from the artist, but for the most part collectible art is purchased through an art dealer, gallery, or auction house. Over the last 50 years, the art market has gone through many cyclical steps, usually in a seven- to ten-year period of rapid appreciation, followed by a pull back to a normal appreciation of around 12 percent. Through these cycles, many collectors have realized gains of up to 200 percent or more in as little as two years! They have also had the reverse happen: purchasing art at a peak and then having to wait a substantial amount of time to recoup their dollars spent. Working with a trusted dealer will guide you through the pros and cons of each purchase, and the wisdom of collecting a particular work will be thoroughly explained.

Over the years of my career, I have represented several artists in selling their original works of art. I have also had innumerable conversations with art dealers about this topic, gaining insight from many who have been in the art business for several generations. Most of the respected galleries and art dealers will tell you to collect art that appeals to you personally, because this criterion always ensures that your investment will pay you the dividends that are most important to you. What is clear, even for the newly rich collector who aspires to own specific artists of yesteryear, is that enormous wealth does not guarantee that those **Monet**, **Picasso**, **Pollock**, **Warhol**, or **van Gogh** paintings will be available. The idea that wealth will bring instant obtainability is often a misconception of some collectors. One soon discovers that he or she is competing with museums and other collectors from around the world who are also in the market for these famous works of art. One can live a comfortable life without the private ownership of such fine art, of course, and the demand for these works is voluntary and determined by means and especially desire.

In his excellent book, *The Value of Art*, published in 2012, ***Michael Findlay***, a renowned art dealer who began his career in 1964, spells out exactly what has transpired in the art market over the last 50 years. It is fascinating! To arrive at the market value of a work of art, the following five attributes must be known and weighed carefully:

Provenance

Condition

Authenticity

Exposure

Quality

When considering all of these points, one must first determine the true motivation for the purchase of a masterpiece. If it is primarily for investment, these five points must be carefully weighed. If the main component is the sheer enjoyment of owning the art, well-respected collectors, as Findlay points out, often make quick, emotional decisions. For instance, he writes about a couple who purchased a **van Gogh** many years ago titled *Adeline Pavoux* (1880) while they were strolling along 57th Street in New York City. The husband explained, "We bought it in ten minutes, for about $11,000. We weren't thinking about investment. We were both struck by its cheerful quality and thought this was the type of picture that would always give us a lift." The collector was Reverend Theodore Pitcarn, and his simple words of praise, "cheerful quality" and "always give us a lift," are at the heart of why someone should choose to own a great painting. Giving pleasure is the true value of art. The rest is icing on the cake.

Many collectors of fine original art explain the euphoria that engulfs them when they stand in front of a great work that elicits strong feelings, boosts their spirits, or changes their mood. This "high" is exactly what the motivation should be for owning original art work. We choose what to put on our walls for many reasons. These include nostalgia, sentimentality, remembrance of loved ones and heroes, both secular and religious. Findlay writes, "After all, 'real' collectors buy what speaks to them and to hell with where it will go." The most serious collectors pay a great deal of attention to how their works of art will decorate their homes. The art they own must fit into their living space while also expressing their own personal taste.

I am an advocate of collecting original art for all of the aforementioned reasons. I also believe that one should not be limited to only buying original art, especially if a collector's desire to own a particular work cannot overcome the fact that it is just not available. Another private collector or a museum might own it. That's where *Prestige Fine Art* comes in. Collecting a spectacular copy of the art desired is another, often equally satisfying, way to go.

As much as I enjoy great master copies, I also have a passion to meet and view mid-career artists and see what their work has to offer. I make it a point to visit as many art events that are of interest to me to stay on the cutting edge of new developments in the field. It is by doing this that I can share my thoughts and opinions gathered from the collectors with whom I work. I have made it known throughout the art world that art is my passion, and it is contagious.

One of the great patrons of postwar American art was Giuseppe Ponza di Biumo, a wealthy Italian. When he died in 2008, his obituary quoted his own words: "I collect art because I love beauty, not to make money." This is a superior reason to explore all avenues of owning art.

## Auction Houses: Sotheby's and Christie's

The two most prominent auction houses are Sotheby's and Christie's. They each conduct major auctions every year, specializing in various artists and styles. In many cases, these auction houses represent the estates of art collectors who have passed on. Art collectors and dealers are very keen on these two auction houses, and they often attend the auctions to bid on works of art that they are interested in acquiring. It is worth noting that approximately half of the art that changes hands annually takes place at the auction houses--the other half changes ownership via private sales and galleries. Anyone who has ever read the terms and conditions stated in the auction house literature knows that at best, "The buyer needs to beware." An enormous amount of marketing goes into promoting the sale of art by these auction houses, which serves to expand the awareness of art and the auction houses' ultimate purpose of attracting sellers and buyers.

## Galleries

I am very familiar with many reputable fine art galleries. They are a wonderful source for viewing, learning about, and purchasing collectible art. Depending on what type of art work a collector is looking for, I have directed or assisted in locating a specific art style or a particular artist's work. Many galleries that I associate with are multigenerational, with the younger family members now running them. They love what they do. Galleries, in some cases, represent an individual artist whom they promote extensively and maintain under contract. There are very high-end galleries that promote living and dead artists, and there are galleries that represent mid-career artists only. No matter what the area of expertise, all of these galleries serve one common purpose: to further the understanding and enjoyment of art.

*Prestige Fine Art* shares that purpose. Our high regard and enthusiasm for great original art is expressed through our desire to honor and recreate these works to the very best of our ability--giving art collectors from all walks of life the opportunity to revel in the pride and pleasure of ownership.

# Our Art Collectors' Homes

EACH OF THE HOMES FEATURED ON THE FOLLOWING PAGES REPRESENTS A UNIQUE CHALLENGE TO ENHANCE THE LIFESTYLE AND SURROUNDINGS OF A PARTICULAR CLIENT, ACCORDING TO HIS OR HER WISHES. SINCE *PRESTIGE FINE ART* HAS THE ABILITY TO PAINT ANY PAINTING IN ANY SIZE, WE CAN TAILOR ALL ART WORK TO SUIT AN ART COLLECTOR'S HOME AND TASTE. THE COLLECTOR SIMPLY CHOOSES HIS FAVORITE MASTERPIECES AND MATCHES THEM WITH OPTIMAL DISPLAY PLACES THROUGHOUT THE HOME. THESE PROJECTS HAVE GIVEN ME THE REWARDING PLEASURE OF HELPING CLIENTS AND/OR THEIR DECORATORS CREATE PERSONALIZED ART MUSEUMS OF THEIR OWN.

# Highland Beach Home

This home owner, an avid art collector and successful businesswoman, wanted us to recreate the Boca Raton home's mood for her beach house. We asked her to let us take the lead and place preliminary art work on the first floor of the home. At *Prestige Fine Art,* we are counted on to add art to the estates of a few collectors per year, so we keep about 200 paintings in inventory for the purpose of "staging" homes—a great way for a client to decide what she likes and doesn't like. Once this particular client made those decisions, we had set the tone on the first floor--and we

**REMBRANDT, PONTORMO, VERMEER**
Office, Study, Room

moved up the staircase to the upstairs bedrooms, offices, and media rooms. The client loved the results. What better compliment is there than a client requesting our services after viewing another client's home. By listening and guiding the customer and sharing our knowledge of great paintings we are able to help create a masterpiece home!

**THE MERMAID,** *by Leighton, Federic*

**ROMEO AND JOILET,**

*Sculpture Artist, unknown*

**DUCAL PALACE, VENICE,**

*by Canaletto*

**GARDEN OF LOVE,**

*by Rubens*

**THE TRIBUNA OF THE UFFIZI**

*by Zoffany, John*

**CEZANNE, EISLEY, MONET,**

guest bedroom

# Atlanta Home

The Atlanta home was a wonderful project for us. *Prestige Fine Art* was presented with the task of finding paintings by several grand masters that depicted African Americans in a meaningful way. I chose **Winslow Homer**'s work and several other artists. The home owner made his own suggestions, too, which we researched to find a fitting selection from which to choose. The collector wanted

THE GULF STREAM, *by Homer, Winslow (top)*

UNCLE NED AT HOME,
*by Homer, Winslow (top)*

our artist to paint eight out of ten select paintings on a large format canvas, 6 x 9 feet. I thoroughly enjoy this kind of project, working with large paintings to make large statements. We delivered the paintings with our white glove treatment and rented scaffolding to double hang the large paintings one above the other. Wow!

DRESSING FOR THE CARNIVAL, *by Homer, Winslow*

PRIDE, *by T.W. Hovenden*

THE BALTIMORE NEWS VENDOR, *by T. W. Hovenden*

MARKET WOMAN, *by T. W. Hovenden*

THE BRIGHT SIDE, 1865, *By Homer, Winslow*

MARKET WOMAN
*by T. W. Hovenden*

TO THE HIGHEST BIDDER, *by Harry Herman Roseland*

A few months later, the collector decided he had room for another five paintings, and I located references for him. He made quick decisions, and we proceeded. There's no better compliment than a satisfied client.

# London Home

This home offered several areas for which we reproduced specific paintings, chosen by the owner from our large photographic album of 500 paintings. This professionally photographed album is designed to make the selection process easy and enjoyable. Once the paintings were picked out by the client, we at *Prestige Fine Art* decided on the most appropriate sizes and frames to suit each display space and the home overall.

ADORATION OF THE MAGI
*by Rubens , Peter Paul*

BUCINTORO RETURNING, *by Canaletto*
PORTRAIT OF A MAN, *by Messini*

DESTINY
*by Waterhouse, John William*

CAVE OF THE STORM NYMPHS
*by Poynter, Sir Edmond John*

**SEAPORT WITH THE EMBARKATION OF THE QUEEN OF SABA**
*by Lorraine, Claude*

**PANDORA**
*by Waterhouse, John William*

**IN THE PERISTYLE**
*by Waterhouse, John William*

**LADY GODIVA**
*by Collier, John (The Honorable)*

# Royal Palm Home

Sometimes my services are called upon by other entrepreneurs to assist with their own work. In this case, a luxury home developer, who owns several large properties in prestigious areas, wanted to stage a home he planned to sell, and he thought fantastic artwork would help him do that. First, he met with me to select paintings in specific sizes from the references I showed him. Then he picked one of our artists to paint all of the chosen works. The open house gathering was grand and included an instrumental quartet to complement the beautiful artwork. The house was sold to an

**THE BROKEN FLOWER POT**
*by Verhas, Jan*

**WILD FLOWERS**
*by Waterhouse, John William*

**THE SODA FOUNTAIN**
*by Glackens, William J.*

**FLOWERS AND FRUIT**
*by Renoir, Pierre Auguste*

**A FRIDAY AT THE SALON OF THE FRENCH ARTISTS**
*by Grun, Jules Alexandre*

**PAINTERS SALON**
*by Stevens, Alfred*

executive and sports team owner from England, and he decided to keep every single painting in the home. Not only that, he ordered a dozen more paintings for his new house.

**FLOWERS AND FRUIT**
*by Renoir, Pierre Auguste*

# Sanctuary Home

**BROTHER AND SISTER**
*by Beechey, Sir William*

**FANTASY FISH BOWL**
*by Goodes*

**GALLEY WITH VIEWS OF MODERN ROME**
*by Pannini, Giovanni Paolo*

In some cases, a collector has a distinct vision of her own. My job is to determine exactly what that vision is so I can help a client realize it. I ask questions about preferred art styles. In many instances, I show examples of several painting styles to assist with a direction. These references come from art books, auction catalogues, or websites, and sometimes I supply large-scale posters and prints so the client can better envision how a painting might look in a specific location. Often the client "lives" with the print for a while to get a better feel. Sometimes "walking away and coming back later" helps with the decision process. This home is one of three that *Prestige Fine Art* filled with paintings,

**BAHAMAS HARBOUR 1882**
*by Bierstadt, Albert*
(painted as vertical, original is horizontal)

**SEAPORT WITH EMBARKATION OF QUEEN OF SABA**

*by Lorraine, Claude*

(painted as vertical original horizontal)

**GRAND CANAL**

*by Turner, William*

**THE PASSAGEWAY OF THE OPERA**

*by Beraud, Jean*

so the client knows our process well. For her, we actually reoriented a horizontal painting into a vertical painting, showing the client sketches first, so she could enjoy a favorite image and still fit it into a vertical spot. The results for this home, and the others we have outfitted for this client, have been outstanding! She obviously thinks so, because we are working on house number four.

**BIRTH OF VENUS**

*by Botticelli, Alessandoa*

**THE LAMENT FOR ICARUS**

*by Draper, Herbert*

199

# Boca Raton Home

We completed this home for a powerful CEO who took charge, knew what he wanted, and selected bold paintings, which reflected his strong character. We started in the living room/entertaining area, and I introduced him to the concept of double and triple hanging a wall (placing two or three paintings on the same wall, above one another). To do this well, one must first determine the subject and style of the art, as well as the best sizes, so everything fits together and creates the most impact. In addition, the framing must be considered

**COURSE OF THE EMPIRE**
*by Cole, Thomas*

**LEIGHTON, DRAPER, COLE,**
*(various artist)*

**COLE, WATERHOUSE, MONET, BERAUD, BOUGUEREAU, MAIGNAN**
Art Collectors Bedroom

**FLAMING JUNE,** *by Leighton, Fredric*
**GUITARS,** *by D' Angelico*
(can be utilized as sculptures)

**A Friday at the Salon of the French Artists**
*by Grun, Jules Alexandre*

**Knight, Monet, Beraud, Bouguereau, Maignan, Alma Tadema**
(side wall art collectors bedroom)

in advance to make sure that the display works with the room and the desired mood. This is a man's home. The client selected predominantly masculine works with hints of romanticism. As I educate my collectors to appreciate great masterpieces, they become better at determining what styles fit their lives and homes. Shortly after completing this home, we began to get inquiries from the owner's guests who liked what they saw. One woman, who owns a beach house, said, "I want my home to have the same feel as his," and we delivered (see Highland Beach Home for the results).

**Lillith**
*by Collier, John*
**A Favorite Custom, and A Difference of Opinion**
*by Alma Tadema*

**A Friday at the Salon of the French Artists**
*by Grun, Jules Alexandre*

# Victoria Park Home

SEASCAPE AT SAINTE-MARIES (VIEW OF MEDITERANEAN)
*by Gogh, Vincent van*

This particular home was both challenging and exciting because the owner wanted to create a fresh and new, very up-to-date contemporary style. We reviewed many artists and paintings that we thought might fit his taste and ultimately selected paintings by **Vincent van Gogh**, whose work is forever new and has a distinctly contemporary feel. We then accented these painting selections with two pastels, also by **Vincent van Gogh**. The collector also wanted some original art by **Al Razza**, a great choice because his work heightened the overall mood perfectly.

SIDEWALK CAFE AT NIGHT
*by Gogh, Vincent van*

**ATTACHMENTS**
*by Razza (original)*

**GUN FIGHT TODAY O. KAYES CORRAL**
*by Kaye, Otis*

**ORCHARD SURROUNDED BY CYPRESSES**
*(Pastel) by Gogh, Vincent van*

**THE SOWER,** *(Pastel) by Gogh, Vincent van*
**FLOWERING ALMOND BRANCH,** *by Gogh, Vincent van*

# Testimonial

FOR OVER 20 PLUS YEARS WE HAVE BEEN CREATING MASTERPIECE PAINTINGS FOR ART COLLECTORS TO ENJOY. ONE OF THE THINGS I LIKE TO DO IS ONCE WE COMPLETE A PROJECT OR HOME FOR A COLLECTOR AND THEY RECEIVE DELIVERY I LIKE TO SPEAK TO THEM. IN THE MAJORITY OF THE CASES I RECEIVE A CALL FROM THEM EXCLAIMING HOW MUCH THEY LOVE AND ADMIRE THE NEW ART WORK THEY NOW HAVE. AS THIS POINT I WILL ASK THEM IF THEY COULD SIT DOWN AND WRITE ME A LETTER DESCRIBING THE EXPERIENCE OF DEALING WITH ME AND *PRESTIGE FINE ART*.

The following letters are a few responses I have received, and I now have over 100. I often comment that they are a feather in my cap.

These letters remind me why I am passionate about what the mission statement at *Prestige Fine Art* stands for and the enjoyment our art work brings to the art collectors we work with.

*Our Mission ?*

*To produce the finest Museum Quality Hand Painted*

*Oil painting re-creations in the world and to satisfy*
*collector's desires and requirements...*

**ARGENTEUIL**
*by Monet, Claude 24 x 20*
Prestige Fine Art

Dear Mr. Mero:

Today we received **Monet's** Cliff Walk….our fourth painting from your fine gallery. It took my breath away. I am so thrilled because it is even lovelier than I imagined.

All of the paintings are so exceptional quality. They look wonderful in our home. I appreciate all the assistance and advice you gave me in selecting the right painting for the right spot. We could not be more pleased. Rest assured, we will call you in the future should we need more art.

Sincerely,

*Mr. & Mrs. H. L. Eidel*

Dear Mr. Mero:

I wanted to let you know how happy we are with our latest painting of "Spring" by **Cot**. Our daughter Michele says it is now her favorite. I tell everyone our 3 paintings from you are like out 3 children, I love each one and have no favorites! "Spring" is such a wonderful compliment in our living room across from "Storm", also by **Cot**. We are so pleased with the frame, it is just perfect with everything else in the room! I am enclosing photos for you to keep. We are also thrilled with "Abduction of Psyche", by Bouguereau, in our Master Suite. We are now looking forward to receiving "Mother and Children", by **Bouguereau**, for our family room.

Edward you have been a joy to work with and we have learned to trust your judgment with the framing. Being the perfectionist that I am, I am not easy to please. Your service is excellent and you go the extra mile, which is almost a lost art in this day and age.

It was so exciting to meet you and visit your gallery. We were impressed with the scope of works you have in stock.

Please feel free to use me as a reference any time. I will be happy to talk with anyone if they would like to call me.

Thank you,

Joyfully,

*Kathy Ivec*

**SPRING**
*by Cot, Pierre Auguste 36 x 24*
*Prestige Fine Art*
Prestige Fine Art

**CLIFF WALK**
*by Monet, Claude 24 x 30*
Prestige Fine Art

**THE STORM**
*by Cot, Pierre Auguste 36 x 24*
Prestige Fine Art

**ABDUCTION OF PSYCHE**
*by Bouguereau, Adolphe William 60 x 33*
Prestige Fine Art

**BROTHER & SISTER**
*by Beechey, Sir William 60 x 48*
Prestige Fine Art

**THE LIBYAN SIBYL**
*by Buonarroti, Michelangelo 40 x 30*
Prestige Fine Art

**"LILITH"**
*by Collier, John (The Honorable) 48 x 24*
Prestige Fine Art

**Dear Edward:**

I would like to take this opportunity to let you know what a pleasure it was dealing with you and your staff at Prestige, but I did not realize how much I would enjoy the experience until I uncrated our painting.

We could never have been more pleased, as the painting is outstanding. I was so excited I just had to hang the painting that evening.

Ben and I have been looking for a painting for our center hall for some time now, and we are glad that we waited and were fortunate enough to find the Prestige Company.

Your artist captured the essence of the original we saw at the Louvre so well, we wished he would have signed it. You have delivered more than anticipated.

Thank you again, and we look forward to our next purchase.

Sincerely,

*Donna & Ben Scheps*

**Dear Mr. Mero:**

For months we looked for just the right piece of art to hang on a wall which is a focal point when entering our new home.

We tried tapestry, but decided that it was too somber. After seeing your ad, we decided to give you a try. Last month we took possession of our painting, "The Libyan Sibyl", and we are absolutely delighted with it. Your artists did an excellent job in reproducing this panel from the Sistine Chapel. Our home is now complete, and we are proud to display this beautiful masterpiece!

We will recommend you without hesitation.

Sincerely,

*Edward S. Shea*

**Dear Ed Mero, and Prestige Fine Art,**

Richard and I are extremely pleased with our purchase from you. You and all of the people at Prestige Fine Art are such a joy with which to work. We will definitely be back to do business again. It is wonderful to come across people that still take pride in their business and service. You combined business, with a friendly, easy going atmosphere that completely put us at ease. As for the artwork, well, it's amazing! We couldn't be happier!

Thank you so much, we just can't say enough good things about the service, and the quality of work regarding Prestige. It was certainly a pleasure.

Sincerely,

*Lesley A. Busch, Vice President*
*Richard C. Busch II, President*

**PANDORA**
*Waterhouse, John William 30 x 20*
Prestige Fine Art

## Suggested Art Books and Movies

ANOTHER PASSION I HAVE ACQUIRED ALONG THE WAY IS THAT I ENJOY READING, VIEWING, AND COLLECTING BOOKS ON ART. AS I TRAVEL AROUND THE GLOBE, I MAKE IT A POINT TO TAKE THE TIME TO VISIT MUSEUM GIFT SHOPS TO PERUSE THEIR SELECTION OF BOOKS ON THEIR EXHIBITIONS AND PERMANENT COLLECTIONS. IT IS NOT UNCOMMON FOR ME TO SPEND HOURS SURVEYING WHAT BOOKS I WILL SELECT. ONCE WHILE VISITING THE LOUVRE & D'ORSAY IN FRANCE, I ACTUALLY HAD TO PURCHASE AN EXTRA LARGE SUITCASE TO ACCOMMODATE THE BOOKS THAT I PURCHASED TO TAKE HOME ON THE PLANE. THE BOOKS ONE FINDS WHILE VISITING THESE MUSEUMS SERVE IN SEVERAL WAYS. THE INDIVIDUAL BOOKS ON THE MUSEUMS' COLLECTION AND/OR THE EXHIBIT ON DISPLAY BECOME A WONDERFUL MEMORY OF THE EXPERIENCE. WHILE SITTING AT HOME REMINISCING, YOU CAN PAGE THROUGH THESE BOOKS AND REVISIT THE ART WORK YOU SO ADMIRED WHEN YOU WHERE THERE!

My personal library is overflowing with choice volumes of art books. Some of the books I have retained are written in French, Italian, not necessarily English. The color plates in these books have been extremely helpful in adding masterpiece paintings to the *Prestige Fine Art* works of art. The jewels one uncovers are astounding--The Courtland Gallery in England, The Barnes Collection in Pennsylvania, The Frick Collection in NYC, etc.--these have all become part of the *Prestige* archives.

Another resource for art education is auction catalogues. Each year Sotheby's and Christie's publish hardback books on their major auctions held that year. These books are packed with color plates and information on the art works sold and pricing, and are available for purchase from all of the major auction houses. A yearly subscription preview of all of their upcoming auctions is also offered and provides the option to order individual magazines on specific areas of art interest. This information allows one to understand what specific styles and paintings are fetching at auction. More importantly, it is another opportunity to view spectacular paintings that very well may end up in private collections tucked away out of sight for years.

I am also an advocate of Sister Wendy, a British nun who has taken the initiative, through her extensive writing, to educate a broad audience on some of the greatest paintings and artists in the world. I fully appreciate the enormous task of compiling accurate and precise information, applaud her for her efforts and have enjoyed many of her books.

*"One of the wonderful things about a museum is how you're jolted into confronting art from strange and wonderful civilizations and you look and learn and expand your horizons."*

*Sister Wendy Beckett*

Sister Wendy's 1000 Masterpieces

Sister Wendy Beckett's selection of the Greatest Paintings in Western Art

One of the very best series on individual artist books that I have found is published by Harry N. Abrams, an American publisher of high-quality art and illustrated books. "Abrams Titles in the Master of Art Series" include numerous volumes that contain over 100 illustrations including 40 full page plates in full color. The series has individual books on over 40 of the great master artists with educational text written by scholars and professors who are experts in their appropriate fields. This series has proven to be an invaluable resource for our art department. In the early years before easy access to computers, we would purchase a complete set of the 40 titles for each of our new art consultants. This resource would be kept readily available at their office for quick reference on masterpiece paintings.

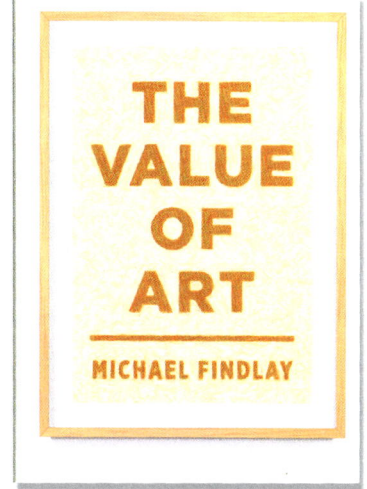

With delight, on my most recent reading of "The Value of Art" by seasoned art dealer Michael Findlay, I came across a chapter which mentions Mr. Abrams admiration for art. Harry believes that it should be part of the office and home network, specifically paintings on the walls, to enhance one's mood and disposition (Chapter 11 Euphrosyne) The Social Value of Art.

In the very early 1960s, Harry Abrams had a friend in the publishing business, John Powers, who ran Prentice Hall. Harry loved contemporary art almost as much as he loved proselytizing. He became determined to share his passion with John, who at first was nonplussed by modern art. Exasperated, Harry sent a group of large colorful paintings by Alfred Jensen to John's office as a long term loan. Sometime later, while visiting Prentice Hall, to his dismay, Harry saw the paintings, in a corridor and still wrapped. "I don't know where to put them" said John; but actually he had plenty of space, he just didn't particularly understand them. Harry grabbed the paintings, found the company cafeteria and hung them himself. "The result was amazing and immediate," John told me many years later. "Everyone in the company had an opinion; some liked them and some loathed them, some were puzzled, and some were delighted; but, everyone spoke up, and the effect on morale was great." (Page 83), "The Value of Art" Michael Findlay.

It is exactly because of stories like these that I am passionate about what we offer here at *Prestige Fine Art*...the chance to lift one's spirits with hand painted copies of art work from past centuries.

Another fine art publisher of books worldwide is Taschen Books. Their ability to explain each artist's painting in an interesting and informative way is a testament to the importance of art in our culture and society. Taschen has taken books on great art, including photography, to a whole new level by creating a series of very large format 28 x 20" hard bound collector books displaying hundreds of expertly reproduced photographs of master photographers such as Helmut Newton, and such. I came across one of these books being displayed on a stand in a small luxurious hotel in Florence, Italy. What a wonderful pastime for guests to be able to browse while enjoying their stay!

This is a partial list of suggested reading and viewing favorites. Additional titles and viewing suggestions can be obtained by visiting museumqualityfineart.com (suggested reading).

## Suggested Movies

Following is a partial list of the educational and inspirational movies depicting artist's lives that I recommend viewing:

Devine Entertainment Corporation "The Artist Series"

**Cassatt, Monet, Degas, Goya, Rembrandt** and **Homer**.

> *"The Artist' specials are whimsically entertaining, richly human mini-dramas that serve as inspiring introduction to great artists for children and their families…Indispensable."*
>
> *Hollywood Reporter*

"The Thomas Crown Affair" - United Artist MGM **Director John McTiernan**, starring **Pierce Brosnan**. Entertaining and amusing story about art work that goes missing from major museum.

"Girl with the Pearl Earring" - Director **Peter Webber**, starring **Scarlett Johansen**, **Colin Firth** and **Tom Wilkinson**. A young peasant maid in the house of the painter Johannes Vermeer becomes his talented assistant and the model for one of his most famous paintings.

The Private Life of a Masterpiece:

This is a BBC arts documentary series which tells the stories behind great works of art; 29 episodes. Some of the art works included are:

**Michelangelo**: David

**Edvard Munch**: The Scream

**Vincent van Gogh**: Sunflowers

**Auguste Renoir**: Bal au Moulin de la Gallette

This is a sampling of the films produced by independent TV production company Fulmar TV. The series producer, who also devised the concept of the program, was Jeremy Bugler.

Many movies and documentary films continue to be produced on artist lives and provide inspiration about their masterpieces. *Prestige Fine Art* will continue to compile and share this information with art lovers around the globe. Visit our website museumqualityfineart.com for suggested book, films, and events area for further information.

# Prestige Fine Art's Museum-Inspired Vision

Walt Disney died in 1966, five years before Walt Disney World opened. When someone said it was sad that Walt Disney had not lived to see the Florida theme park, Mike Vance, creative director of Walt Disney Studios, replied, "He did see it; that is why it's here." Dreams do not happen just because you want them to, you must hang in there, be tenacious--stick to it--until you are finally able to turn your dreams into a reality.

*--From The Success Secrets of Walt Disney*

*by Pat Williams*

Stirred by these words, and after countless years spent working with artists, collectors, art dealers, galleries, and studying the great masters through art books and especially museums, I have seen an exciting vision of my own: building a Museum of Great Museums, an art center that will represent the culmination of the world's greatest art. It will not be static. Like language, art lives and breathes, and the art center would reflect this idea with ongoing classes, video links, high-tech interactive features, books, lectures, and art exhibitions.

I have been carrying around this dream for years, and I have had a lifetime to hone the details. My goal is to expand the concept of making exquisite fine art copies--to the supreme recreation of the great museums that house the art that inspires them. Our museum center will be built on 100 acres of land to allow room to grow. The structure of the building will incorporate the facades of each of ten of the world's greatest museums, and I imagine an approximate 100,000 square foot overall building. Inside, the must-see art works of each of the ten museums will be on display-- excellent copies, of course. And the walls of the interior spaces will duplicate the interiors of each of the ten museums,

with at least one room dedicated to each. Think of a Russian nesting doll, each one tucked into the other. The large main building will showcase what I call museum spirit, the essence of what museums are all about. The rooms inside will honor the individual museums, and the smaller "dolls" would be the works of art themselves. Ultimately, the museum center will become a place for art lovers to visit and linger, to better grasp the meaning of museums as monuments to the past and present, while giving them imaginative glimpses of the future of museums and art--all this as they wander from place to place around a grand campus.

As the great museums of the world are undergoing ambitious remodeling to meet contemporary museum standards or blending neoclassical and modern (think the glass pyramid at the Louvre), others are leveraging the wonderful technological and architectural abilities of the 21st century (think the Guggenheim in Bilbao, Spain). Still other impressive museums haven't even been built yet, but the plans and models tell us that these institutions will lead us to amazing prospects (think the proposed museum in Dubai). Our center will be ultra-imaginative and futuristic while preserving the greatness of the past, and it will take full advantage of the mobile, virtual, and interactive technology of the present. Art movies will be played on large IMAX screens on rotating schedules, depicting the lives of the great artists, living and dead. We might even create an area that replicates **Monet**'s Garden at Giverny, France--a timeless oasis of artistic inspiration brought to you, instead of you traveling to it.

Our museum-inspired center would also be a fabulous learning center. Art classes will be taught by skilled instructors to stimulate budding artists and older art lovers. Text books and e-books would be at every student's disposal. We would plan annual events to attract audiences from around the world, encouraging an eclectic exchange of ideas. One idea is to create our own Pageant of the Masters (which celebrates its 80th anniversary this year in Laguna Beach, California), the famous "colored chalk on the sidewalk" contest. Maybe our pageant will use the exterior sides of the museum walls as a unique canvas for our competing muralists!

Traveling exhibits of original art by artists from countries around the globe would also be highlighted. Interactive displays for individuals

**THE NATIONAL GALLERY OF ART**
*Washington DC USA*

**THE LOUVRE MUSEUM**
*Paris, France*

**"GALLERY OF THE GREAT MUSEUMS OF THE WORLD"**
*Drawing of building architectural façade.*
*The National Gallery of Art and The Louvre Museum*
*(northeastern view of building)*

with interest in the arts will be developed and incorporated into a computer network, which would include iPads and large computer screens. A research library, both actual and virtual, will provide everything you need to know about art history and the great masters. Part museum, part educational center, and part technology hub, our museum center will become a renowned celebration of art, a go-to resource, and an awesome and beautiful place to wallow in the awesome beauty of the museums and art that feed our civilization's soul.

**THE ART INSTITUTE OF CHICAGO**
*Chicago ILL USA*

**THE METROPOLITIAN MUSEUM OF ART**
*New York City NY USA*

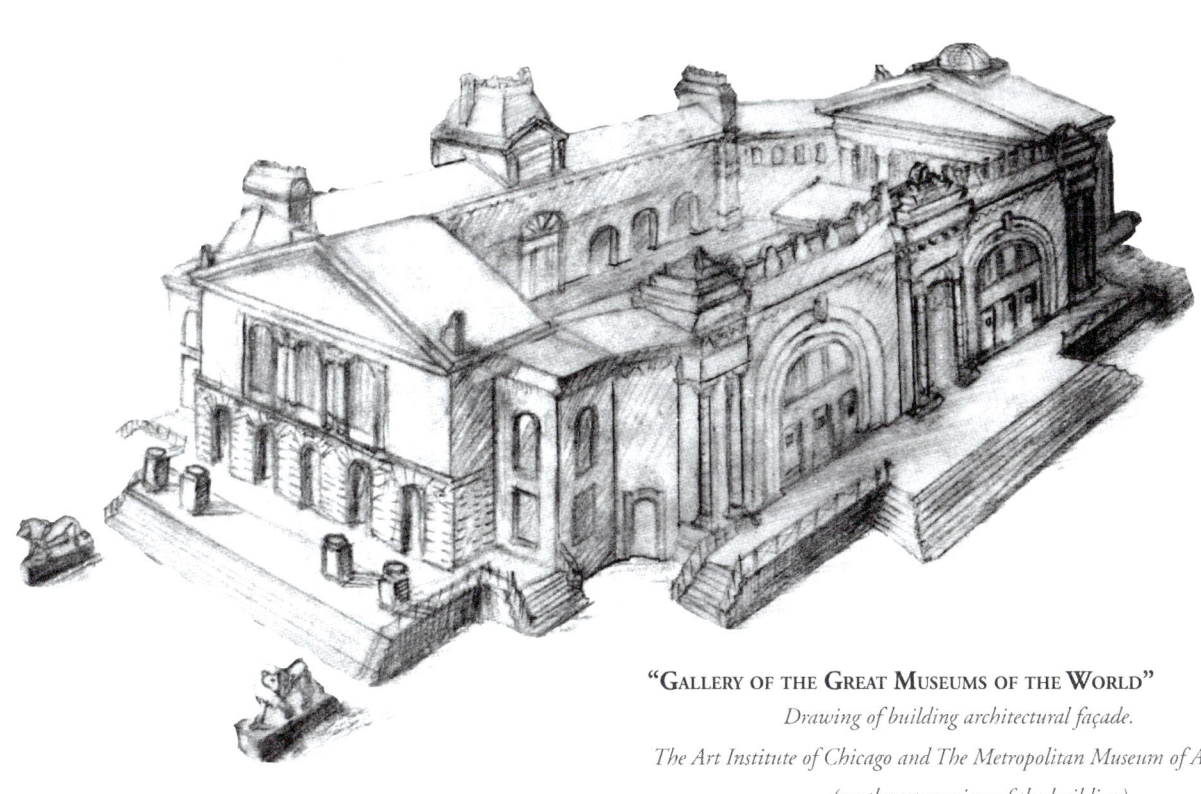

**"GALLERY OF THE GREAT MUSEUMS OF THE WORLD"**
*Drawing of building architectural façade.*
*The Art Institute of Chicago and The Metropolitan Museum of Art*
*(southwestern view of the building)*

215

*Funding for* **"The Gallery of the Great Museums of the World"**
*will come from art lovers around the world.*

*To be part of the project visit* **www.MuseumQualityFineArt.com**
*and pledge your support.*

*Prestige Fine Art* strives to be synonymous with the term, museum quality. Our hope is that when you view our paintings as a cohesive body of work, you come away with the collective power of past and present artists and the masterpieces that they produce.

As we move into the future, we want to expand our reach, not only through the artwork we produce for hundreds of individual collectors, but through our own, interactive art campus—our museum-inspired vision and this author's long-held dream.

You can become an important part of *Prestige Fine Art*'s Museum-Inspired Vision through your contributions. To learn more about this exciting project intended for art lovers around the world, visit Museumqualityfineart.com and pledge your support.

The masterworks of the next generations might look different than those of the past, but one thing will never change: the artist's desire to conceive ideas and create art, and humanity's need to appreciate art and remember.

# Index

## A

### ART COLLECTORS HOMES

Adoration of the Magi - *by Rubens , Peter Paul* **194**

A Favorite Custom, and A Difference of Opinion - *by Alma Tadema* **201**

A Friday *at the Salon of the French Artists - by Grun, Jules Alexandre* **197, 201**

Attachments - *by Razza (original)* **203**

Bahamas Har*bour* **1882 - by Bierstadt, Albert 198**

Birth of Venus - *by Botticelli, Alessandoa* **199**

Brother and Sister - *by Beechy, Sir William* **198**

Bucintoro Returning - *by Canaletto* **194**

Cave of the Storm N*ymphs - by Poynter, Sir Edmond John* **194**

Cole, Waterhouse, Monet, Beraud, Bouguereau, Maignan - Art Collectors Bedroom **200**

Course of the Empire - *by Cole, Thomas* **200**

Destin*y - by Waterhouse, John William* **194**

Dressing for the Carnival - *by Homer, Winslow* **192**

Ducal Palace, Venice - *by Canaletto* **191**

Fantas*y Fish Bowl - by Goodes* **198**

Flaming June - *by Leighton, Fredric* **200**

Flowering Almond Branch - *by Gogh, Vincent van* **203**

Flowers and Fruit - *by Renoir, Pierre Auguste* **197**

Galle*y with Views of Modern Rome - by Panni, Giovanni Paolo* **198**

Grand Canal - *by Turner, William* **199**

Guitars, *by D'Angelico* **200**

Gun Fight Toda*y O. Kayes Corral - by Kaye, Otis* **203**

In the Perist*yle - by Waterhouse, John William* **195**

Lady *Godiva - by Collier, John (The Honorable)* **195**

Lillith - *by Collier, John* **201**

Market Woman - *by T. W. Hovenden* **193**

Orchard Surrounded *by Cypresses - by Gogh, Vincent Van* **203**

Painters Salon - *by Stevens, Alfred* **197**

Pandora - *by Waterhouse, John William* **195**

Portrait of a Man - *by Messini* **194**

Razza **203**

Seaport with Em*barkation of Queen of*

Saba - *by Lorraine, Claude* **199**

Seaport with the Em*barkation of the Queen of Saba - by Lorraine, Claude* **195**

Seascape at Sainte-Maries (View of Mediteranean) - *by Gogh, Vincent van* **202**

Sidewalk Cafe at Night - *by Gogh, Vincent van* **202**

The Baltimore News Vendor - *by T. W. Hovenden* **193**

The Bright Side, 1865 - B*y Homer, Winslow* **193**

The Broken Flower Pot - *by Verhas, Jan* **196**

The Gulf Stream - *by Homer, Winslow (top)* **192**

The Lament for Icarus - *by Draper, Herbert* **199**

The Mermaid - *by Leighton,Federic* **190**

The Passagewa*y of the Opera - by Beraud, Jean* **199**

The Soda Fountain - *by Glackens, William J.* **196**

The Sower - *by Gogh, Vincent van* **203**

The Tri*buna of the Uffizi - by Zoffany, John* **191**

To the Highest Bidder - *by Harry Herman Roseland* **193**

Uncle Ned at Home - *by Homer, Winslow (top)* **192**

Wild Flowers - *by Waterhouse, John William* **196**

### ARTIST

Alma Tadema **201**

Alma-Tadema, Sir Lawrence **99, 113, 141, 142**

Beeche*y, Sir William* **169**

Beech*y, Sir William* **198**

Bellini, Giovanni **170**

Benoist, Marie-Guillemine **66**

Benson, Frank Weston **127**

Beraud **201**

Beraud, Jean **125, 127, 199**

Bierstadt, Al*bert* **156, 158, 198**

Bloch, Carl Heinrich **148**

Bogdan*y, Jakob* **133**

Bonheur, Rosa **58**

Bonvicino, Alessandro **170**

Bosschaert, Am*brosius (The Elder)* **72, 113**

Botticelli, Alessandoa **199**

Botticelli, Alessandro di Mariano Filipepi **116**

Boucher, Francois **61, 95**

Bouguereau **200, 201**

Bouguereau, Adolphe William **110, 140, 142, 169, 171**

Breton, Jules Adolphe Aime Louis **87**

Bronzino, Agnolo **90, 118**

Buttersworth, James Edward **154**

Caille*botte, Gustave* **86, 126**

Canaletto **191, 194**

Canaletto (Giovanni Antonio Canal) **133, 136**

Caravaggio **117, 171**

Cassatt, Mary **127**

Cezanne **191**

Cezanne, Paul **79, 85, 104, 105, 127**

Cham*bers, George* **150**

Charlemont, Eduard **139**

Cole **200**

Cole, Thomas **158, 200**

Collier, John (The Honora*ble)* **139**

Consta*ble, John* **91, 98, 101**

Corot, (Jean-Baptiste) Camille **80**

Cot, Pierre Auguste **59, 61**

Co*ypel, Antoine* **78**

Co*ypel, Noel-Nicolas, (detail)* **81**

Co*ypel, Noel-Nicolas, (extended)* **81**

D' Angelico **200**

David, Jacques-Louis **68, 143, 151**

Degas, Edgar **80, 124, 162**

de Heem, Jan Davidz **138**

Delacroix, Eugene **66, 138**

da Vinci, Leonardo **67, 146**

Dicksee, Sir Frank **139**

Draper **200**

Draper, Her*bert* **99, 199**

Durand, Asher Brown **157**

D*yce, William* **148, 169**

D*yck, Sir Anthony Van* **169**

Edward Moran **159**

Eisle*y* **191**

Elsle*y, Arthur John* **170**

Fragonard, Jean-Honore **92, 93, 138, 139**

Gains*borough, Thomas* **171**

Garden of Love - *by Rubens* **191**

Gates, H. L **171**

Gauguin, Paul **107**

Gerard, Francois **171**

Gerome, Jean-Leon **59**

Giovanni Antonio **117**

Gogh, Vincent van **110, 128, 202, 203**

Gogh,Vincent van **162**

Goodes **198**

Go*ya, Francisco* **14**

Greuze, Jean Baptise **69, 168**

Grun, Jules Alexandre **124, 201**

Harnett, William Michael **73, 154**

Harry *Herman Roseland* **193**

Hassam, Frederick Childe **159**

Ha*yter, George* **169**

Heade, Martin Johnson **157**

Homer, Winslow **72, 156, 192**

Hovenden, Thomas **155**

Hu*ysum, Jan van* **112**

Ingres, Jean-Auguste Dominique **66, 90**

Jean-Honore Fragonard  67
John William  194
Knight  201
Knight, Daniel Ridgway  156
Krafft, Barbara  169
Lawrence, Sir Thomas  171
Lebrun, Charles  135
Lefebvre, Jules Joseph  86
Leighton  200
Leighton,Federic  190
Leighton, Frederic--Lord of Stretton  138
Leighton, Frederic-Lord of Stretton  171
Leighton, Fredric  200
Lewis, John Federick  102
Liotard, Jean-Etienne  113
Lorraine, Claude  132, 199
Maignan  200, 201
Manet, Edouard  14, 59, 67, 87, 126
Messina, Antonello da  170
Metsys, Quentin  68
Millet, Jean-Francois  132, 133
Modigliani, Amedeo  59, 171
Monet  191, 201
Monet Beraud  200
Monet, Claude  59, 60, 67, 72, 73, 74, 75, 88, 126, 129
Moran Edward Percy  146
Moran, Thomas  156, 157
Morisot, Berthe  74, 85
Murillo, Bartolome  116, 132
Palmer, Samuel  99, 101
Pannini, Giovanni Paolo  134
Peale, Charles Willson  168
Peale, Rembrandt  168
Peter Paul  194
Pissarro, Camille  127
Pontormo  190
Pontormo, Jacopo Carucci  111
Potthast, Edward Henry  85
Poynter, Sir Edmond John  194
Prendergast, Maurice  156
Prestige Fine Art  165, 166, 167, 172
Raphael  119
Rembrandt  190
Rembrandt Harmensz, van Rijn  90, 132, 133, 164, 170
Rembrandt, Harmensz, van Rijn  73, 118
Rembrandt Peale  168
Remington Frederic  147
Remington, Frederic  148, 149
Reni, Guido  143
Renoir, Pierre August  106
Renoir, Pierre Auguste  58, 73, 78, 84, 126, 127, 129, 197
Riggiani  141
Rousseau, Henri  104
Rubens  191
Rubens, Peter Paul  132, 133, 134
Ruisdael, Jacob van  111
Russell, Charles M  149

Sargent, John Singer  100, 157
Scrotes, Guillim  170
Seurat, Georges  84, 105, 107
Smith, John Brandon  157
Stevens, Alfred  197
Story, G. H  168
Stubbs, George Townly  98
Tapiro y Bara, Jose  138
Theodore Gericault  69
Tintoretto, Jocopo Robusti  150
Tissot, James Jacques Joseph  75
Trumbull, John  168
Turner, J.M.W.  60
Turner, William  100, 199
Turner,William  102
T.W. Hovenden  192
Vanaise, Gustave  169
Vanderlyn, John  168
Verhas, Jan  196
Vermeer  190
Vermeer, Jan  59, 67, 73, 91, 132, 133, 136, 139
Vroom, Hendrick Cornelisz  147
Wardle, Arthur  138
Waterhouse  200
Waterhouse, John William  195, 196
Winterhalter, Xavier  171
Winterhaulter Franz  164, 168
Zoffany, John  135, 191

# C

## CATEGORIES

### Americana  159

A Rocky Torrent - Grand Canyon - by Moran, Thomas  156

Bahamas Harbour, 1882 - by Bierstadt, Albert  158

Grand Canyon with Rainbow - by Moran, Thomas  157

Kindred Spirits - by Durand, Asher Brown  157

Mrs. Fiske Warren and Her Daughter Rachel - by Sargent, John Singer  157

Old Models - by Harnett, William Michael  154

Pride - by Hovenden, Thomas  155

Sierra Nevada - by Bierstadt, Albert  156

Snap the Whip - by Homer, Winslow  156

South Boston Pier - by Prendergast,

Maurice  156

Study of an Orchid - by Heade, Martin Johnson  157

Taking His Ease, 1885 - by Hovenden, Thomas  155

Tending the Rose Garden - by Knight, Daniel Ridgway  156

The Avenue in the Rain - by Hassam, Frederick Childe  159

The Consummation of Empire (Course of the Empire Series) - by Cole, Thomas  158

The Old Violin - by Harnett, William Michael  154

The Yacht Magic Defendaing America's Cup, 1870 - by Buttersworth, James Edward  154

Three Boys in Lobster Boat - by Homer, Winslow  156

Waterfall - by Smith, John Brandon  157

### Historical and Western

A Dash for the Timbers - by Remington Frederic  147

Attack on the Supply Wagons - by Remington, Frederic  149

Bombardment of Algiers - by Chambers, George  150

Bonaparte Crossing the Alps - by David, Jacques-Louis  151

Defeat of the Spanish Armada - by Vroom, Hendrick Cornelisz  147

In Without Knocking - by Russell, Charles M  149

Justice - by Anonymous  151

Loops and Swift Horses are Surer than Lead - by Russell, Charles M  149

Napoleon Addressing the Second Corp of the Grand Army - by Gautherot, Pierre  148

Neptune Resigning to Britannia the Empire of the Sea - by Dyce, William  148

The Ambush - by Russell, Charles M.  149

The Battle of Waterloo, 1815 - Prestige Fine Art **148**

The Capture Constantinople - *by Tintoretto, Jocopo Robusti* **150**

The Cinch Ring - *by Russell, Charles M.* **149**

The Last Supper - *by da Vinci, Leonardo* **146**

The Sermon on the Mount - *by Bloch, Carl Heinrich* **148**

The Trooper - *by Remington, Frederic* **149**

Washington Reading his Farewell Address - *by Moran Edward Percy* **146**

When the Law Dulls the Edge of Chance - *by Russell, Charles M.* **148**

## Impressionism

Argenteuil - *by Monet, Claude* **126**

Breakfast in Bed - *by Cassatt, Mary* **127**

Calm Morning - *by Benson, Frank Weston* **127**

Chez Le Pere Lathuile - *by Manet, Edouard* **126**

Dans la prairie - *by Monet, Claude* **126**

Monet Painting in His Garden in Argenteuil - *by Renoir, Pierre Auguste* **127**

Nature Morte:les Grosses Pommes - *by Cezanne, Paul* **127**

Outside the Theater du Vaudeville (Emulation) - *by Beraud, Jean* **127**

Paris Street Scene (Emulation) - *by Beraud, Jean* **125**

Sailing Boat at Argenteuil - *by Caillebotte, Gustave* **126**

Seascape at Sainte-Maries (View of Mediteranean) - *by Gogh, Vincent* **128**

Sidewalk Cafe at Night - *by Gogh, Vincent van* **128**

Spring Bouquet - *by Renoir, Pierre Auguste* **126**

The Apple Seller - *by Renoir, Pierre Auguste* **129**

The Dinner Party (Emulation) - *by Grun, Jules Alexandre* **124**

The Duck Pond - *by Monet, Claude* **129**

The Gardens of Les Mathurins at Pontoise, 1876 - *by Pissarro, Camille* **127**

The Passageway of the Opera - *by Beraud, Jean* **125**

The Pink Dancers - *by Degas, Edgar* **124**

The Two Sisters - *by Renoir, Pierre Auguste* **126**

## Old Master Old World

Adoration of the Magi - *by Rubens, Peter Paul* **132**

Bucintoro Returning to the Molo On Acension - *by Canaletto (Giovanni Antonio Canal)* **136**

Fruit and Birds - *by Bogdany, Jakob* **133**

Grand Canal The Rialto Bridge from the North - *by Canaletto (Giovanni Antonio Canal)* **133**

Seaport with the Embarkation of the Queen of Saba - *by Lorraine, Claude* **132**

Shepherds with Her Flock - *by Millet, Jean-Francois* **132**

St. Michael - *by Murillo, Bartolome* **132**

The Allegory of Painting - *by Vermeer, Jan* **136**

The Angelus - *by Millet, Jean-Francois* **133**

The Astronomer - *by Vermeer, Jan* **133**

The Crowning of Saint Catherine - *by Rubens, Peter Paul* **133**

The Return of the Prodigal Son - *by Rembrandt Harmensz, van Rijn* **133**

The Storm on the Sea of Galilee - *by Rembrandt Harmensz, van Rijn* **132**

The Tribuna of the Uffizi - *by Zoffany, John* **135**

The Triumph of Alexander - *by Lebrun, Charles* **135**

Woman with a Pearl Necklace - *by Vermeer, Jan* **132**

## Pastels

Dancers at the Barra, 1877-79 - *by Degas, Edgar* **162**

Danseuse - *by Degas, Edgar* **162**

Les Ballerines - *by Degas, Edgar* **162**

Orchard Surrounded by Cypresses - *by Gogh, Vincent van* **162**

The Sower - *by Gogh, Vincent van* **162**

Young Woman wiaa Dancer with Tambourine - *by Degas, Edgar* **162**

## Portraits

A Boy Reading (Titus) - *by Rembrandt Harmensz, van Rijn* **170**

Abraham Lincoln - *by Story, G. H* **168**

A Girl with a Basket of Fruit - *by Leighton, Frederic-Lord of Stretton* **171**

Aristotle Contemplating the Bust of Homer - *by Rembrandt Harmensz, van Rijn* **170**

Art & Literature, 1867 - *by Bouguereau, Adolphe William* **169**

Brother & Sister - *by Beechey, Sir William* **169**

Conway Wedding Portrait - *by Prestige Fine Art* **165**

Daisies - *by Bouguereau, Adolphe William* **169, 171**

Empress Josephine of France #2 - *by Gerard, Francois* **171**

George Washington - *by Peale, Rembrandt* **168**

Henry Howard, Earl of Surrey - *by Scrotes, Guillim* **170**

Her New Love - *by Elsley, Arthur John* **170**

Jesus Christ - *by Prestige Fine Art* **169**

John Adams - *by Peale, Charles Willson* **168**

La Peinture en Plein Air - *by Vanaise, Gustave* **169**

Philadelphia and Elizabeth Wharton - *by Dyck, Sir Anthony Van* **169**

Pinkie - *by Lawrence, Sir Thomas* **171**

Portrait of a Knight of Malta - *by Caravaggio* **171**

Portrait of a Man - *by Messina, Antonello da* **170**

Portrait of a Woman with Black Tie - *by Modigliani, Amedeo* **171**

Portrait of a Young Man - *by Bellini, Giovanni* **170**

Portrait of a Young Man - *by Bonvicino, Alessandro* **170**

Portrait of Benjamin Franklin - *by Greuze, Jean Baptise* **168**

Portrait of Donald Trump - *by Prestige Fine Art* **172**

Portrait of Elly - *by Prestige Fine Art* **172**

Portrait of Elmer and Natalie Mero - *by Prestige Fine Art* **172**

Portrait of Jacquie Mero - *by Prestige Fine Art* **172**

Portrait of James Kenny - *by Prestige Fine art* **172**

Portrait of James Madison - *by Vanderlyn, John* **168**

Portrait of Lavoisier - *by Prestige Fine Art* **167**

Portrait of Louis Pasteur - *by Prestige Fine Art* **167**

Portrait of Marie Curie - *by Prestige Fine Art* **167**

Portrait of Mark & JoAnn Skousen with son at Machu Picchu - *by Prestige Fine Art* **166**

Portrait of Mr. & Mrs. DeRosa - *by Prestige Fine Art* **172**

Portrait of Mrs. Osherow - *by Prestige Fine Art* **172**

Portrait of Mrs. van Spall - *by Prestige Fine Art* **172**

Portrait of Nicole and Jacquie Mero - *by Prestige Fine Art* **172**

Portrait of Sam Houston - *by Prestige Fine Art* **168**

Portrait of the Etzel Children - *by Prestige Fine Art* **172**

Portrait of The Latham's - *by Prestige Fine Art* **172**

Portrait of Thomas Edison - *by Prestige Fine Art* **167**

Portrait of Tracy & Brittany - *by Prestige Fine Art* **172**

Portrait of Tyler Perry - *by Ron DiScenzi* **172**

Portrait of Wolfgang Amadeus Mozart - *by Krafft, Barbara* **169**

Portriat of the Trout Family - *by Prestige Fine Art* **172**

Prince Albert - *by Winterhaulter Franz* **168**

Queen Victoaria at her Coronation, 1838 - *by Hayter, George* **169**

Royal Family - *by Winterhaulter Franz* **164**

Self-Portrait as a Young Man - *by Rembrandt Harmensz, van Rijn* **170**

Self-Portrait at the Age of 34 - *by Rembrandt Harmensz, van Rijn* **164**

Self Portrait John Trumbull - *by Trumbull, John* **168**

Sir Arthur Conan Doyle - *by Gates, H. L* **171**

The Blue Boy - *by Gainsborough, Thomas* **171**

The First of May, 1851 - **by Winterhalter, Xavier** **171**

The Meeting of Jacob and Rachel - *by Dyce, William* **169**

Thomas Jefferson - *by Rembrandt Peale* **168**

**Romantic Classical Victorian**

Abduction of Psyche - *by Bouguereau, Adolphe William* **140**

A Sculpture Gallery - *by Alma-Tadema, Sir Lawrence* **142**

Aurora - *by Reni, Guido* **143**

Banquet Still Life with Parrots - *by de Heem, Jan Davidz* **138**

Circe - *by Wardle, Arthur* **138**

Lady Godiva - *by Collier, John (The Honorable)* **139**

Mars Disarmed *by Venus and the Three Graces - by David, Jacques-Louis* **143**

Preparations For The Marriage of the Sherif's Daughters - *by Tapiro y Bara, Jose* **138**

Rest, 1879 - *by Bouguereau, Adolphe William* **140**

Romeo & Juliet - *y Dicksee, Sir Frank* **139**

Song of the Angels, 1881 - *by Bouguereau, Adolphe William* **142**

The Guitar Player - *by Vermeer, Jan* **139**

The Lion Hunt - *by Delacroix, Eugene* **138**

The Mermaid - p*by Leighton, Frederic--Lord of Stretton* **138**

The Musical Contest - *by Fragonard, Jean-Honore* **139**

The Recital - *by Riggiani* **141**

The Stolen Kiss - *by Fragonard, . Jean-Honore* **139**

The Swing - *by Fragonard, Jean-Honore* **138**

Unconscious Rivals - *by Alma-Tadema, Sir Lawrence* **141**

Vermeer in His Studio - *by Charlemont, Eduard* **139**

# F

## FLOWERS AND FRUIT - BY RENOIR, PIERRE AUGUSTE 197

# M

## MUSEUMS

The Art Institute of Chicago

A Holiday - *by Potthast, Edward Henry* 85

Bridge Over Waterlillie Pond - *by Monet, Claude* 88

Bullfight in Spain - *by Manet, Edouard* 87

Marseilles, Seen from l' Estaque - *by Cezanne, Paul* 85

Odalisque - *by Lefebvre, Jules Joseph* 86

On the Terrace - *by Renoir, Pierre Auguste* 84

Paris Street, Rainy *Day* - *by Caillebotte, Gustave* 86

Sunday *Afternoon on the Island of La Grande Jatte* - *by Seurat, Georges* 84

The Song of the Lark - *by Breton, Jules Adolphe Aime Louis* 87

Water Lilies, 1906 - *by Monet, Claude* 88

Woman at her Toilett - *by Morisot, Berthe* 85

## The Barnes Collection

Beach Scene, Guernse - *by Renoir, Pierre August* 106

Entrance to the Port of Honfleur - *by Seurat, Georges* 107

Haere Pape - *by Gauguin, Paul* 107

Leda and the Swan - *by Cezanne, Paul* 104

Models - *by Seurat, Georges* 105

The Card Pla*yers (*2) - **by Cezanne, Paul** 105

The Promenade - *by Renoir, Pierre Auguste* 106

Woman Walking in an Exotic Forest - *by Rousseau, Henri* 104

## The Frick Collection

Autumn - *by Boucher, Francois* 95

Comtesse d'Haussonville - *by Ingres, Jean-Auguste Dominique* 90

Girl Interrupted At Her Music - *by Vermeer, Jan* 91

Lodovico Capponi - *by Bronzino, Agnolo* 90

Self-Portrait - *by Rembrandt Harmensz, van Rijn* 90

Spring - *by Boucher, Francois* 94

Summer - *by Boucher, Francois* 94

The Flute Player - *by Boucher, Francois* 95

The Love Letters - *by Fragonard, Jean-Honore* 92

The Lover Crowned - *by Fragonard, Jean-Honore* 92

The Pursuit - *by Fragonard, Jean-Honore* 93

The Rendezvous - *by Fragonard, Jean-Honore* 93

The White Horse - *by Constable, John* 91

Winter - *by Boucher, Francois* 95

## The J. Paul Getty Museum

Basket of Flowers, 1614 - *by Bosschaert, Ambrosius (The Elder)* 113

Cosimo I de'Medici - *by Pontormo, Jacopo Carucci* 111

Dutch Still Life: Flowers and Fruit - *by Huysum, Jan van* 112

Irises - *by Gogh, Vincent van* 110

Portrait of Maria Fredke van Reede-Athlone at Seven Years - *by Liotard, Jean-Etienne* 113

Spring - *by Alma-Tadema, Sir Lawrence* 113

Two Watermills with an Open Source - *by Ruisdael, Jacob van* 111

Vase of Flowers - *by Huysum, Jan van* 112

Young Girl defending Herself Against Eros - *by Bouguereau, Adol-*

*phe William* 110

## The Louvre

Grande Odalisque - *by Ingres, Jean-Auguste Dominique* 66

Officer of the Imperial Guard - *by Theodore Gericault* 69

Portrait of a Negress, Salon of 1800 - *by Benoist, Marie-Guillemine* 66

Portrait of Mona Lisa - *by da Vinci, Leonardo* 67

The Astronomer - *by Vermeer, Jan* 67

The Bolt - *by Jean-Honore Fragonard* 67

The Broken Pitcher - *by Greuze, Jean Baptise* 69

The Coronation of Napoleon and Josephine - *by David, Jacques-Louis* 68

The Fifer - *by Manet, Edouard* 67

The Money *Lender and His Wife* - *by Metsys, Quentin* 68

Wild Poppies - *by Monet, Claude* 67

Women of Algiers in Their Apartment - *by Delacroix, Eugene* 66

## The Metropolitan Museum Of Art

Garden at Sainte-Adresse - *by Monet, Claude* 60

In the Meadow - *by Renoir, Pierre Auguste* 58

Landscape The Parc Monceau *by Monet, Claude* 59

Pygmalion and Galatea - *by Gerome, Jean-Leon* 59

Reclining Nude - *by Modigliani, Amedeo* 59

Spring - *by Cot, Pierre Auguste* 59

The Artist's Garden, Versailles - *by Manet, Edouard* 59

The Grand Canal, Venice - *by Turner, J.M.W.* 60

The Horse Fair - *by Bonheur, Rosa* 58

The Storm - *by Cot, Pierre Auguste* **61**

Toilette of Venus - *by Boucher, Francois* **61**

Young Girls at the Piano *by Renoir, Pierre Auguste* **58**

Young Girls at the Piano - *by Renoir, Pierre Auguste* **58**

Young Woman with a Water Jug *by Vermeer, Jan* **59**

### The National Gallery of Art

A Summer's Day - *by Morisot, Berthe* **74**

Bouquet of Flowers in a Glass Vase - *by Bosschaert, Ambrosius (The Elder)* **72**

Bouquet of Flowers in a Glass VaseThe National Gallery *of Artby Bosschaert, Ambrosius (The Elder)* **72**

Breezing Up (A Fair Wind) - *by Homer, Winslow* **72**

Cattle*ya Orchid and Three Brazilian Hummingbirds - by Heade, Martin Johnson* **73**

Hide and Seek - *by Tissot, James Jacques Joseph* **75**

Oarsmen at Chatou - *by Renoir, Pierre Auguste* **73**

The Artist's Garden at Vetheuil - *by Monet, Claude* **72**

The Bridge at Argenteuil - *by Monet, Claude* **73**

The Girl with a Red Hat - *by Vermeer, Jan* **73**

The Japanese Foot*bridge - by Monet, Claude* **74**

The Old Violin - *by Harnett, William Michael* **73**

The Return Of The Prodigal Son - *by Rembrandt, Harmensz, van Rijn* **73**

Woman with a Parasol Madame Monet and Her Son - *by Monet, Claude* **75**

### The Philadelphia Museum Of Art

Abduction of Europa - *by Coypel,Noel-Nicolas,(detail)* **81**

Abduction of Europa - *by Coypel,Noel-Nicolas,(extended)* **81**

Antibes Morning - *by Monet, Claude* **79**

Bacchus and Ariadne on the Isle of Naxos - *by Coypel,Antoine* **78**

Mont Sainte-Victoire - *by Cezanne, Paul* **79**

Mother Protecting Child - *by Corot, (Jean-Baptiste) Camille* **80**

The Bathers - *by Renoir, Pierre Auguste* **78**

The Mante Family - *by Degas, Edgar* **80**

### The Tate Gallery

A Favourite Custom - *by Alma-Tadema, Sir Lawrence* **99**

A Hil*ly Scene - by Palmer, Samuel* **101**

Bridge of Sighs - *by Turner, William* **100**

Carnation Lil*y, Lily Rose - by Sargent, John Singer* **100**

Mares and Foals in a River Landscape - *by Stubbs, George* **98**

The Court*yard of the House of Coptic - by Lewis,John Federick* **102**

The Gleaning Field - *by Palmer, Samuel* **99**

The Gle*be Farm - by Constable,John* **98**

The Grove Hampstead - *by Constable, John* **101**

The Lament for Icarus - *by Draper, Herbert* **99**

The Waterfalls, Pistil Mawdduch, North Wales - *by Palmer, Samuel* **101**

Venice, Bridge of Sigh - *by Turner,William* **102**

### Uffizi & Pitti Gallery

Bacchus - *by Caravaggio* **117**

Birth of Venus - *by Botticelli, Alessandro di Mariano Filipepi* **116**

Ducal Palace, Venice - Canaletto, Giovanni Antonio **117**

La Donna Velata - *by Raphael* **119**

Portrait of Angelo Doni - *by Raphael* **119**

Portrait of Isa*belle de'Medici - by Bronzino, Agnolo* **118**

Self-Portrait as a Young Man - *by Rembrandt, Harmensz, van Rijn* **118**

Virgin with a Rosary - *by Murillo, Bartolome* **116**

## P

### PHOTOGRAPHY AND PHOTOREALISM

Clown Fish - *by Mike Poirier* **183**
Clown Fish in Coral - *by Mike Poirier* **183**
display *Art & Photography Books - by Taschen* **182**
Lionfish in coral - *by Mike Poirier* **183**
Longjaw Squirrelfish with Coral wall - *by Mike Poirier* **183**
Taschen Collector *book signed - by Helmut Newton* **182**

## S

### SCULPTURE

A Friday *at the Salon of the French Artists - by Grun, Jules Alexandre* **173**
Ballerina II - *by Canova, Antonio* (1757-1822) **174**
Eric's Creations **175**
In a mar*ble cave - by Nilda Maria Comas* **178**
Life B, 2000 mar*ble height* **25"Life B, 2000 marble height 25" by Nilda Maria Comas by Nilda Maria Comas 178**
Love and P*syche - by Canova, Antonio* (1757 - 1822) **174**
Mecury - *by Bologna, da Giovanni* **174**
Melancolia 2000 mar*ble - by Nilda Maria Comas* **179**
Palm Beach Girl 1998 *bronze - by Nilda*

*Maria Comas* **178**
Pieta - *by Michelangelo* **177**
*Pygmalion and Galatea - by Gerome,
Jean-Leon* **174**
The Kiss - *by Rodin, Auguste* **174**
Victory, **1999 - by Nilda Maria Comas
179**

## T

### TESTIMONIAL

Brother & Sister - *by bBeechey, Sir William*
**207**
Cliff Walk - *by Monet, Claude* **206**
Lilith - *by Collier, John* **207**
Pandora - Waterhouse, John William **207**
Spring - *by Cot, Pierre Auguste* **206**
The Li*byan Siby - pby Buonarroti,
Michelangel* **207**
The Storm - *by Cot, Pierre Auguste* **206**

*Funding for* **"The Gallery of the Great Museums of the World"**
*will come from art lovers around the world.*

*To be part of the project visit* **www.MuseumQualityFineArt.com**
*and pledge your support.*

# Edward Mero – *Prestige Fine Art*

**Edward Mero** is an internationally recognized art dealer with a creatively driven passion for the arts. Born in Anchorage, Alaska, he is the co-author of *The Secret of Freedom*. He lives in South Florida and maintains a residence in New York City, but his expansive approach is inspired by the world at large.

Made in the USA
San Bernardino, CA
19 August 2013